SHAKESPEARE AND THE BIBLE.

AMS PRESS
NEW YORK

Shakespeare and the Bible.

TO WHICH IS ADDED

PRAYERS ON THE STAGE,

PROPER AND IMPROPER.

SHAKESPEARE'S USE OF THE SACRED NAME OF

D E I T Y.

THE STAGE VIEWED FROM A SCRIPTURAL AND
MORAL POINT. THE OLD MYSTERIES AND
MORALITIES THE PRECURSORS

OF THE

ENGLISH STAGE.

BY

JAMES REES,

AUTHOR OF "THE LIFE OF EDWIN FORREST," "DRAMATIC
AUTHORS OF AMERICA," "FOOTPRINTS OF
A LETTER-CARRIER," ETC.

"We ought to make collection of the thoughts of Shakespeare, that
they may be cited on every occasion, and under every form; and no man
who has a tincture of letters can open his works without finding there a
thousand things which he ought not to forget."—*Villemain.*

PHILADELPHIA:
CLAXTON, REMSEN & HAFFELFINGER,
624, 626 & 628 MARKET STREET.
1876.

Library of Congress Cataloging in Publication Data

Rees, James, 1802-1885.
    Shakespeare and the Bible.

    Reprint of the 1876 ed.
    1. Shakespeare, William, 1564-1616--Knowledge--
Bible. 2.   Theater--Moral and religious aspects.
I. Title.
PR3012.R4 1972   822.3'3   70-174307
ISBN 0-404-05235-5

Reprinted from an original copy in the collections of the
George Peabody Department of the Enoch Pratt Free Library

From the edition of 1876, Philadelphia
First AMS edition published in 1972
Manufactured in the United States of America

AMS PRESS INC.
NEW YORK, N. Y.   10003

THIS VOLUME

Is Dedicated by its Author

FRANCIS H. DUFFEE, ESQ.,

AS

A SLIGHT TRIBUTE

OF A

Long and Lasting Friendship.

v

SHAKESPEARE AND THE BIBLE, are the two great sources from whence mankind have realized more of the truths of religion, and of the laws by which men and nations are governed, than all others combined. The Bible is the word of God, hence it is a divine revelation, and those who do not consider it in that light, view it only as an historical work, and live and die as men do without a belief of the great future. The Bible needs no champion ; it is the light that shines into the soul, as the sun shines upon the earth, vivifying all beneath its influence, and should either withdraw its radiance, both recipients would suffer.

Shakespeare has given us a vast amount of intellectual wealth — he is quoted at the bar, the rostrum, and the pulpit — his original thoughts and ideas have become familiar to us through the medium of the stage, but many of his bright and beautiful gems have shone for ages in different forms in that sacred volume, which contains the revelations of God, the Scriptures of the Old and New Testament. How much Shakespeare was indebted to the Bible for many of his most beautiful passages, and how beneath his hand the gems of old were set anew, and to what extent he made use of his knowledge to aid him in the production of plays, it is our purpose to show.

Perhaps there are no other works extant that more closely follow that great stream of truth and knowledge, which flows through the pages of the Bible, than those of Shakespeare. As an evidence of which, we quote the following, as one of the most striking illustrations of our subject which is to be found in history :

" The Bible and Shakespeare," said one of the best and most esteemed prelates that ever sat upon the English bench— Dr. John Sharp, in the reign of Queen Anne — " The Bible and Shakespeare have made me Archbishop of York."

BIBLE.

" This book — this holy book, on every line
　　Mark'd with the seal of high divinity ;
　　On every leaf bedew'd with drops of love
　　Divine ; and with the eternal heraldry
　　And signature of God Almighty stampt
　　From first to last — this ray of sacred light,
　　This lamp from off the everlasting throne,
　　Mercy took down, and in the night of time
　　Stood, casting on the dark, her gracious brow."

Robert Pollok.

SHAKESPEARE.

" Who now shall grace the glowing throne,
    Where, all unrivalled, all alone,
Bold Shakespeare sat, and look'd creation through,
The minstrel monarch of the worlds he drew ?
That throne is cold — that lyre in death unstrung,
On whose proud note delighted wonder hung,
Yet old oblivion, as in wrath he sweeps,
One spot shall spare — the grave where Shakespeare sleeps.
Rulers and ruled in common gloom may lie,
But Nature's laureate bards shall never die,
Art's chiselled boast, and glory's trophied shore,
Must live in numbers, or can live no more.
While sculptured Jove some nameless waste may claim,
Still rolls th' olympic car in Pindar's fame ;
Troy's doubtful walls, in ashes passed away,
Yet frown on Greece in Homer's deathless lay ;
Rome slowly sinking in her crumbling fanes,
Stands all immortal in her Maro's strains : —
So, too, yon giant empress of the isles,
On whose broad sway the sun forever smiles,
To Time's unsparing rage one day must bend,
And all her triumphs in her Shakespeare end."

Charles Sprague.

CONTENTS

NOTE.— All the quotations from Shakespeare given in this work are taken from the old editions, many from the folio of 1623. Some of the modern editions, termed " acting copies," differ in many instances from the original, not only in the use of words, but in the punctuation, thereby changing the true meaning, as well as the sense, of a whole passage.

SHAKESPEARE AND THE BIBLE.

INTRODUCTORY.

"Hark! hark! the lark at heaven's gate sings."
CYMBELINE.

THE age in which Shakespeare lived was not, in
the strictest sense, an age of morals. Some of
the most prominent men of that period, among whom
were several of the poet's contemporaries, fell victims
to many of the prevailing vices of the day. The
reticence of Shakespeare is one of the reasons historians assign for their limited knowledge of his domestic
habits. He came to London at a period most dangerous to youth, particularly to one who had committed some youthful indiscretion that seemed to
foreshadow his future destiny. Shakespeare's life
while in London affords no evidence to connect him
with scenes of debauchery and wild extravagance.
One or two stories are told of him, but as they are

2   13

unsupported by any positive evidence, they fall to the ground, "the weak invention of the enemy." Shakespeare came to London with a heart that had "been warmed by sitting at a good man's table," and an intellect lighted by the Promethean flame of genius. With these powerful incentives to good actions and the attainment of the object of his youthful aspirations — fame and fortune — he was well prepared to go forth into the world, "and meet the ups and downs of life in no sullen spirit." Shakespeare was not strictly what is called a religious man — he possessed at least sufficient respect for the church and all good men, to rank among the most moral of the age. Schlegel, the great German critic, speaking of Shakespeare, says : "Though the world of spirits and of nature had laid all their treasures at his feet, in strength, a demigod, in profundity of view, a prophet, in all-seeing wisdom a protecting spirit of a higher order, he yet lowered himself to mortals, as if unconscious of his superiority, and was as open and unassuming as a child." "I loved the man," said Ben Jonson, "and do honor his memory on this side idolatry, as much as any. He was, indeed, honest, and of an open and free nature." And Rowe is equally enthusiastic in his praise, and tells us "that every one who had a true taste of merit and could distinguish men, had generally a just value and esteem for him, that his exceeding candor and good nature must certainly have inclined all the gentler part of the world to love him." Another very fascinating feature

in the character of Shakespeare, was the almost constant cheerfulness and serenity of his mind. *"He
was verie good company,"* says Aubrey, "and of a
very ready and pleasant and smooth witt."

There appears to be a gap of seven or eight years in
the life of Shakespeare, which the most learned and
astute commentators have not been able to fill. That
Shakespeare did not consume these years in idle debauchery, is evident from the fact that his greatest
enemy, Robert Greene, does not allude to this vacuum
in the poet's life. The evidence, to the contrary of
time misspent, is to be found in his subsequent productions, wherein is displayed his knowledge of history, art, and science, only to be acquired by close
application and study. If these years in his young
life were devoted to "women, wine, and wassail,"
at what period, then, did he acquire a knowledge of
"law, medicine, history, and the Bible"? That he
was a diligent and a devout reader of the word of
God, and that he had turned this reading to far better
account than any of his critics, we will endeavor to
show. A writer says: "His marvellous knowledge
of the Book of Nature is admitted on all hands; his
knowledge of the Book of Grace, though far less
noticed, will be found, I believe, to have been scarcely
less remarkable. His works have been called 'a sec-
ular Bible.'" In Singer's edition of Shakespeare,
published in 1826, he very quaintly says in his preface:
"It has been remarked that Shakespeare was habitu-
ally conversant with the Bible." Judging from this,

we should say that Mr. Singer had not made this discovery himself, but derived the information from
others.   Shakespeare lived and flourished at the same
time, and under the same reign, with the translators
of what is called "King James' Bible," and it became his text-book and great moral instructor.

In this connection let us quote a few passages from
the admirable remarks of Mr. Knight on Shakespeare
and his plays.   Speaking of the free grammar-school
at Stratford-upon-Avon, founded by a native of the
town, in the reign of Henry VI., and celebrated as
"*the school of Shakespeare*," he says : — "The only
qualifications necessary for the admission of a boy
into the grammar-school of Stratford were, that he
should be a resident in the town, of seven years of
age, and able to read.   The grammar-school was
essentially connected with the corporation of Stratford, and it is impossible to imagine that when the
son of John Shakespeare became qualified for admission to a school where the best education of the time
was given, literally for nothing, his father in that
year being chief alderman, should not have sent him
to the school."

Thither, it is held, Shakespeare, born at Stratford in
1564, went about the year 1571.   Mr. Knight continues :

"Assuredly the worthy curate of the neighboring
village of Luddington, Thomas Hunt, who was also
the school-master, would have received his new
scholar with some kindness.   As his 'shining morn-

ing face' first passed out of the main street, into that old court through which the upper room of learning was to be reached, a new life would be opening upon him. The humble minister of religion who was his first instructor has left no memorials of his talents or acquirements; and in a few years another master came after him, Thomas Jenkins, also unknown to fame. All praise and honor be to them; for it is impossible to imagine that the teachers of William Shakespeare were evil instructors, giving the boy ' husks instead of wholesome aliment.' ''

Shakespeare was what, at this day, is called "a lively boy," full of fun and frolic, one who enjoyed a joke and ever ready to make one. One of the favorite amusements of the boys at that period, was the stealing of "deer and conies." This violation of the rights of property must not, however, be estimated with the rigor which would at the present day be attached to a similar offence. In those ruder days, the spirit of Robin Hood exercised a certain influence over "romantic youth," and deer and coney stealing was classed with robbing orchards, and other adventurous but ordinary levities of youth. It was considered in the light of an indiscretion rather than of a criminal offence; and in this particular the young men of Stratford were countenanced by the practice of the students of the universities. In these hazardous exploits Shakespeare was not backward in accompanying his comrades. The person in whose neighborhood, perhaps on his property, these encroachments were

2 *   B

made, was of all others the individual from whose hands they were least likely to escape with impunity in case of detection.

Sir Thomas Lucy was a Puritan, and one not likely to extend indulgence to the excesses of Shakespeare and his companions; hence, upon his discovering their iniquities, they fell under the lash of the law, and the poet revenged himself by sticking satirical verses on the knight's park. These verses — ten in number, containing forty lines — were not only severe, but personal, to the extent of what would constitute, in our day, just cause for a libel suit. We have selected the following as a fair specimen of the whole:

> " A parliament member, a justice of peace,
> At home a poor scarecrow, in London an asse ;
> If Lucy is Lowsie, as some volke miscall it,
> Synge Lowsie Lucy whatever befall it.

>   .   .   .   .

> " Sir Thomas was too covetous,
>   To covet so much deer;
> When horns enough upon his head
>   Most plainly did appear.
> Had not his worship one *deer* left ?
>   What then ? He had a wife,
> Took pains enough to find him horns
>   Should last him during life."

The *severity* of these verses, added to that inflicted upon their author by Sir Thomas, induced "the gentle Shakespeare" to fly "his native country."— What great results not unfrequently arise from the indiscretions of youth, and their punishment. The Shakespeare of Stratford, became the Shakespeare of the world !

At Stratford, then, at the "free grammar-school" of his own town, Mr. Knight assumes Shakespeare to have received, in every just sense of the word, the education of a scholar. This, it is true, is described by Ben Jonson as "of little Latin and less Greek." Fuller states that his learning was very little, and Aubrey says "that he understood Latin pretty well." Mrs. Griffith, in her excellent work entitled "The Morality of Shakespeare's Drama," says: "It would be an invidious reflection on our poet's fame to suppose him to have been a scholar. A genius *leads* thoughts, a scholar but *borrows* them" [1777].

As to French, it is certain he did not deal with translations only ; for the last line of one of his most celebrated passages, "The Seven Ages of Man," in "As You Like It," is imitated from a poem, called the "Henriade," which was first published in 1594, in France, *and never translated.* Garnier, the author of it, is describing the appearance of the ghost of Admiral Coligny, on the night after his murder, at the massacre of St. Bartholomew, and introduces the following passage :

"*Sans pieds, sans mains, sans nez, sans oreilies, sans yeux, Meurtri de toutes parts.*"

The verse of Shakespeare :

"*Sans teeth, sans eyes, sans taste, sans everything.*"

To assume that William Shakespeare did not stay long enough at the grammar-school of Stratford to obtain a very fair proficiency in Latin, with some knowledge of Greek, is to assume an absurdity upon the face of circumstances. Of Shakespeare's life immediately after his quitting Stratford little is positively known. Collier concurs with Malone, in thinking, that after Shakespeare quitted the "free school" he was employed in the office of an attorney. Proofs of something like a legal education are to be found in many of his plays, and it may safely be asserted that the law phrases do not occur so frequently in the dramatic productions of any of his cotemporaries. His knowledge of medicine may have been derived from serving a few months or so with a village apothecary, and his military information from being a short period a soldier. Aurder, speaking upon this subject, says: "The name William Shakespeare occurs in a certificate of the names and arms of trained soldiers — trained militia, we should now call them — in the hundred of Barlichway, in the county of Warwick, under the hand of Sir Fulk Greville (friend to Sir Philip Sidney), Sir Edward Greville, and Thomas Spenser. Was our William Shakespeare a soldier? Why not? Jonson was a soldier, and had slain his man. Donne had served in the Low Countries. Why not Shakespeare in arms? At all events, here is a field for inquiry and speculation. The date is September 23, 1605, the year of the Gunpowder Plot, and the lists were probably prepared through instructions issued by Cecil in consequence of secret information as to the working of the plot in Warwickshire — the proposed head-quarters of the insurrection."

Questions have arisen how Shakespeare obtained so much knowledge of foreign countries. Mr. Halliwell and Mr. C. Armitage Brown assert that Shakespeare made an Italian journey. It is, however, pretty certain that he visited Venice, Verona, and Florence. At that particular period there was a prevailing rage for foreign travel, and it extended itself to authors and actors. So little is known of the private movements of Shakespeare, that it may be said his travels were a part of his social mysteries. We admit that we are without sufficient evidence to prove a negative, and he may have gone there without having left behind him any distinct recorded fact. At the date to which we are now adverting, he might certainly have had a convenient opportunity of so doing, in consequence of the temporary prohibition of dramatic performances. The suspension commenced a short time before Spenser wrote his " Tears of the Muses," in which he notices the *silence of Shakespeare.* We have no means of ascertaining how long the order inhibiting theatrical performances generally was persevered in ; but the plague broke out in London in 1592, and in the autumn of the year, when the number of deaths was greatest, " the Queen's players," in their progress round the country, whither they wandered when thus prevented from acting in the metropolis, performed at Chesterton, near Cambridge. The more popular members of the theatrical profession, and authors, were entirely lost sight of until the final restoration of the health of the city, and the rescinding of the prohibition.

The plague continued to rage in the autumn of 1593, and Michaelmas term was held, in consequence, at St. Alban's. The following regulation was presented to the Privy Council : — "*That for avoyding of great concourse of people, which causeth increase of the infection, it were convenient that all Playes, Bearebaytinge, Cockpitts, common Bowling Alleyes, and such like unnecessarie assemblies, should be suppressed during the time of infection, for that infected people after thus long keepinge in, and before they be cleered of their disease and infection, being desirous of recreation, use to resort to such assemblies, where through heate and thronge they infect many sound personnes.*"

James I. evinced his strong disposition to favor theatrical amusements, some years before he succeeded to the English throne ; he was a poet himself, or at least had royal pretensions to that distinction. As an evidence of his partiality to the players and stage plays, he, with his own hand, wrote a letter to Shakespeare in return for the compliment paid him in his tragedy of Macbeth. Another evidence of King James's fondness for theatricals, is found in the fact that he was attended during his journey to the north by a regular company of players. It would

seem as if the King did this as a memorial to the
memory of Shakespeare—the bard died April 23, 1616,
and the King's visit to Scotland was in July, 1617.
James was also accompanied by "the children of the
chapel," and "singing men," which goes to
strengthen our belief that he surrounded himself
with players for the purpose of retaining their great
master's memory, by producing his plays, and sur-
rounding his court with all that appertained to theatrical amusements. In 1617, there was a grand feast at
court, given in honor to "the Muscovy ambassa-
dors," on which occasion there was a great display
of beauty and nobles of the court. Ben Jonson's
"Vision of Delight" was performed, with great ap-
plause. It may be said that the reign of Elizabeth
and James not only gave rise to the English drama,
which has become a part of the literary character of
the world, but gave a Shakespeare to rule and govern
that of the "mimic," which, like that of monarchy
itself, has become hereditary — for no other name
than that of Shakespeare's governs it now. Changing
a passage in "Daniel's Defence of Rhyme" by a
word or two, how applicable they are to Shakespeare
in the above connection : "So natural *in his melody*,
and so universal as it seems *to pervade* all nations of
the world, it becomes an hereditary eloquence proper
to all mankind."

Although King James was a great admirer of
Shakespeare, and held his memory as a sacred trust,
he did not forget the Bible, for even at that period

Shakespeare and the Bible were almost synonymed. Shortly after he had succeeded to the English throne, at a conference of divines held at Hampton Court in 1603, James expressed a strong opinion on the importance of having a correct version of the Holy Bible, in consequence of the many imperfections of the existing translations of the Scriptures. "I wish," said he, "some special pains were taken for a uniform translation, which should be done by the best learned in both universities, then revised by the bishops, presented to the Privy Council, and lastly ratified by royal authority, to be read in the whole church, and no other."

Out of this speech of the king's arose the present English Bible, which has now for nearly two hundred and seventy years been the Bible universally used in dissenting communities. It was originally (1611) published under the following title:

"*The Holy Bible, conteyning the Old Testament and the New newly translated out of the original Tongues, and with the former translations diligently compared and revised, by his Majesty's special commandments.*"

We have said that a gap of several years in the life of Shakespeare has not been accounted for. Shakespeare's Day-Book, posted up in the great ledger (folio) 1623, fully explains this mystery. It informs us how this gap was filled up and his time occupied. Let a learned writer speak for us : —

" During such a period of observation Shakespeare

might spend a few weeks or months in different voca-
tions, one after the other ; and, if domiciled with an attorney, an apothecary, or of any other calling, he would
learn more of those arts in six months than he found
occasion in after years to put in his dramas. Let us,
therefore, intelligently, admire Shakespeare's varied
knowledge of the common affairs of life, by considering his vast capacity, in connection with the fact that
this knowledge of his, at which we are so much aston-
ished, is of that kind and degree that comes from observation, and not by any special study or daily practice.''

In the year 1865, Charles W. Stearns, M.D., of
New York, published a small work, entitled "Shakespeare's Medical Knowledge.''

In 1859, there was published by D. Appleton & Co.,
a volume of 146 pages, entitled "Shakespeare's Legal
Acquirements Considered,'' by John Lord Campbell,
LL.D. It is in the form of a letter addressed to J.
Payne Collier, Esq., F.S.A.

Following the example of these learned gentlemen,
we have endeavored, by a series of parallel passages,
to show that his knowledge of the Bible was fully
equal, if not far surpassing, that of his medical and
legal acquirements. Attempts have been made by
some writers to connect Shakespeare's name with that
of the Catholic faith. There is not a particle of evidence to support this. Whether his father was or was
not a member of the Protestant Reformed Church, it
is not to be disputed that his children, all of whom
were born between 1533 and 1580, were baptized at

3

the ordinary and established place of worship in the parish. That his son William was educated, lived, and died a Protestant, we have no doubt, the evidence of which is to be found in several of his plays.

We have in our possession an engraving of the font used at the christening of Shakespeare. It is but a fragment — the upper part only. The same style was adopted with singular good taste for the new font in the church, which may therefore be considered as a restoration of it. Mr. Knight has thus given its history : " The parochial accounts of Stratford show that about the middle of the seventeenth century a new font was set up. The beautiful relic of an olden time, from which William Shakespeare had received the baptismal water, was, after many years, found in the old chancel-house. When that was pulled down, it was thrown into the church-yard, and, half a century ago, was removed by the parish-clerk to form a trough of a pump at his cottage. It was bought by the late Captain Saunders, and from his possession came into that of the present owner, Mr. Heritage, a builder at Stratford." It is still in possession of the family.

The life of William Shakespeare was an extraordinary one, and in the contemplation of it we are lost in wonder and surprise. It is seldom the historian has to record instances of such locomotive powers of genius springing from an humble source, and of one who obtained in so short a time a position in the world of letters, which has never been equalled.

He planted in the garden of literature new and

rare plants; they bloomed in all their pride of
beauty, and perfumed with their sweets the civilized
world. The wilderness yielded its gloom and silence
to his power, and notes of sweet music, conjured up
by his art, are now heard wherever the foot of civilization treads — his, was the magic of the heart, the pulsa-
tion of which harmonized with that of the earth, and
they throbbed together in unison. It was the glory
of Columbus that he discovered a new world for Cas-
tile and Aragon; but Shakespeare has discovered a
new universe — a universe of truth and beauty for the
contemplation of mankind in every age. Life, with
its stern realities, the realms of fancy peopled by genii
and fairies; Nature in all her grandeur, and art in its
refinement, are all presented to us in his writings
encircled by the attributes of genius.

Charming in youth, instructive in age, he addresses
himself to all — he has a voice for every human feeling—he is, in fact, the universal teacher. The Abbé Le
Blanc, in his letters on the English nation, written to
his friend, speaking of Shakespeare, says: "He is, of
all writers, ancient or modern, the most of an original.
He is truly a great genius, and Nature has endowed
him with powers to show it. His imagination is rich
and strong; he paints whatever he sees, and embel-
lishes whatever he describes. The Loves in the train
of Venus are not represented with more grace in the
pictures of Albanus, than this poet gives to those that
attend on Cleopatra, in his description of the pomp
with which that queen presents herself to Mark Antony, on the banks of the Cydnus."

Is it not strange that a poor boy, who came to London a total stranger, should become the master spirit of the world of letters; the magician to rule the minds of men, and give to every nation a key to unlock the prison-doors of ignorance, and bid it forth to learn the words of wisdom? But so it was. He was a link-boy about the theatres, then a "call-boy," then an actor, author, and finally the Shakespeare of all time. But here let us pause, and ask the question, where did he get his biblical knowledge? where did he receive the first lessons which led him on, step by step, to become in time one of the best students of the Bible in his day? Was it while acting in the capacity of a "link-boy," or was it while engaged within the walls of a theatre? No! He received those lessons from one whose love added a bright charm to the holy passages she taught him to read and study — to his mother was Shakespeare indebted for early lessons of piety, and a reverence for a Book, from whose passages in after life, he wove for himself a mantle of undying fame. She lived in an age when books were rare things in the dwellings of the poor; he lived in an age when the Bible was looked upon as the "Book of Books," and read for the good things it contained, and not for the purpose of controversy, as, we regret to say, is in a great measure the case at the present day.

In arranging our passages from Shakespeare, parallel with those of the Bible, we have not given them in the order of the folio edition of his plays (1623), but as they presented themselves in our reading and researches.

WAS SHAKESPEARE A ROMAN CATHOLIC?

THE silly attempt of a few Papist writers to connect Shakespeare with the Catholic Church has totally failed to command a single consideration from those entertaining views of a more liberal faith. There is not a single passage in his writings, or in the records of his life, that indicate his having held the Roman Catholic faith, and it may be fully presumed that, had he held that persuasion, he would not have exposed himself to the censure of that priesthood, by expressing the strong *anti-popish* sentiments conveyed in the following extracts. An old writer, alluding to these passages in the several plays of Shakespeare, says: "A reference to these extracts, it is presumed, that every mind capable of judging will be fully convinced that Shakespeare was not a *Papist*, and it must be borne in mind that the evidence in proof thereof is given by himself—a testimony more powerful than the arguments of commentators."

3 *

No *Papist* would have been inclined, or would have dared, to have put into the mouths of *dramatis personæ*, such expressions, *counter to Papacy*, as are presented in the extracts we now furnish :

KING JOHN, Act III., Sc. I.

K. Philip.— Here comes the holy legate of Rome.

[*Enter* PANDULPH.]

Pandulph.— Hail, you anointed deputies of heaven.
To thee, King John, my holy errand is.
I, Pandulph, of fair Milan, Cardinal,
And from Pope Innocent the legate here,
Do in his name religiously demand,
Why thou against the Church, our holy mother,
So wilfully dost spurn ; and, force perforce
Keep Stephen Langton, chosen Archbishop
Of Canterbury, from the Holy See? . . .

K. John.—What earthly name to interrogatories
Can task the free breath of a sacred king?
Thou can'st not, cardinal, devise a name
So slight, *unworthy and ridiculous,*
To charge me to an answer, as the *Pope.*
Tell him this tale ; and from the mouth of England,
Add thus much more,— that no Italian priest
Shall tithe or toll in our dominions.

.   .   .   .

So tell the Pope ; all reverence set apart
To him, and his usurp'd authority.

K. Philip.— Brother of England, you blaspheme in this.

K. John.— Though you, and all the kings of Christendom,
Are led so grossly by this meddling priest,
Dreading the curse that money may buy out,
And by the merit of vile gold, dross, dust,

Purchase corrupted pardon of a man,
Who, in that sale, sells pardon from himself;
Though you, and all the rest, so grossly led,
This juggling witchcraft with revenue cherish;
Yet I, alone, do me oppose
Against the Pope, and count his friends my foes.
    Pandulph.— Then by the lawful power that I have,
Thou shalt stand cursed and excommunicate."

In the first part of King Henry VI. our readers
will find the following (Act i., Scene 3) — a scene
between Winchester and Gloster :

    Win.— " How now, ambitious Humphrey ! What means this ?
    Glos.— Piel'd priest, dost thou command me to be shut out ? *
    Win.— I do, thou must usurping proditer,
And not protector, of the king and realm.
    Glos.— Stand back, thou manifest conspirator ;
Thou that contriv'dst to murder our dear lord ;
Thou that giv'st whores indulgence to sin.†
I 'll canvas thee in thy broad cardinal's hat,
If thou proceed in this thy insolence.
    Win.— Nay, stand thou back ; I will not budge a foot.
This be Damascus ; be thou cursed Cain,‡
To slay thy brother Abel, if thou wilt.
    Glos.— I will not stay thee, but I 'll drive thee back.

---

 * " Piel'd priest." Piel'd is what is now usually spelled peel'd, and in the
folio of 1623 the orthography is *pield*. It occurs in the same sense in
" Measure for Measure." The allusion is to the shaven crown of the Bishop
of Winchester.

 † The public stews in Southwalk were under the jurisdiction of the
Bishop of Winchester. In the office book of the court all fees were entered
that were paid by the keepers of these brothels — the church reaping the
advantages of these pests to society.

 ‡ " This be Damascus, be thou cursed Cain," etc. In " The Travels of
Sir John Mandeville," we find this passage : " And in that place, where
Damascus was founded, Kayn sloughe Abel his brother."

Thy scarlet robes, as a child's bearing cloth,
I 'll use to carry thee out of this place.

   Win.— Do what thou dar'st.   I 'll beard thee to thy face.

   Glos.— What !   Am I dar'd and bearded to my face'?
Draw, men, for all this privileged place;
Blue coats to tawny coats.*   Priest, beware your beard,

   [*Gloster and his men attack the bishop.*]

I mean to tug it, and cuff you soundly.
Under my feet I stamp thy cardinal's hat,
In spite of pope or dignities of church ;
Here by the cheeks I drag thee up and down.

   Win.— Gloster, thou 'lt answer this before the pope.

   Glos.— Winchester goose ! † I cry — a rope ! a rope !
Now bear them hence ; why do you let them stay ?
Thee I 'll chase hence, thou wolf in sheep's array.
Out, tawny coats ! out, scarlet hypocrite." ‡

     . . . " The cardinal is more haughty than the devil."

                    1 *Henry VI.*, i. 3

   " Name not religion, for thou lov'st the flesh,
     And ne'er, throughout the year, to church thou go'st,
     Except it be to pray against thy foes."

                    1 *Henry VI.*, i. 1.

     . . . " That devil monk
     Hopkins, that made the mischief.

---

  * Tawny coats were worn by the attendants of the Bishop. Stow, in a
passage quoted by Stevens, speaks on one occasion of the Bishop of London, who was " attended on by a goodly company of gentlemen in tawny
coats."   Gloster's men wore blue coats.

  † " Winchester goose."   That the reader may better understand the
terrible words of Gloster addressed to the Bishop and the insult aimed at
his church, the word goose was a particular stage of the disease contracted
in the stews.   Hence Gloster bestows the epithet on the Bishop in derision
and scorn, referring to his licentious life so strongly painted in Act. iii.,
Scene 1, of this most extraordinary play. .

  ‡ We have no doubt but Shakespeare introduced these terrible passages
against the Church of Rome to please Queen Elizabeth, she having been
trained up in a hatred of Popery.

> . . . That was he
> That fed them with his prophecies."
>
> *Henry VIII.*, ii. 1.

"These cardinals trifle with me: I abhor
This dilatory sloth, and *tricks of Rome*."

Henry VIII., ii. 4.

> . . . "I'll startle you
Worse than the sacring bell, when the brown wench
Lay kissing in your arms, Lord Cardinal."

Henry VIII., iii. 2.

"Out of mere ambition, you have caus'd
Your *holy hat* to be stamp'd on the king's coin."

Henry VIII., iii. 2.

"The paper has undone me: 'Tis the account
Of all the world's wealth I've drawn together
For mine own ends: indeed, to gain the *popedom*,
And fee my friends in *Rome*." *Henry VIII.*, iii. 2.

"This is the cardinal's doing — the King Cardinal,
The blind priest,— the king will know him one day."

Henry VIII., ii. 2.

"Oft have I seen the haughty cardinal,
More like a soldier than a man o' the church,
As stout and proud as he were lord of all,
Swear like a ruffian." *2 Henry VI.*, i. 1.

There are numerous other passages all tending to show the author's sentiments in regard to the Church of Rome, as well as his thorough belief and reverence of the Protestant faith. This is exemplified in the similitude of his religious sentences to the passages drawn from the Bible and the liturgy of the Church of England.

C

PARALLEL PASSAGES OF THE PLAYS OF SHAKESPEARE, WITH THOSE OF THE BIBLE, BIBLICAL TEXTS, ETC.

WE stated in our introduction that in arranging the parallel passages of Shakespeare's plays with those of the Bible, it was not our intention to give them in the order of the folio edition of his plays, published in 1623. We will, therefore, commence our series with "The Tempest," one of the most finished productions of the immortal bard.

The general idea of "The Tempest" is taken from the account of St. Paul's shipwreck on the island of Melita, or at least that portion of it speaking of the shipwreck and the island, as mentioned in Acts xxvii. and xxviii. Prospero says to Miranda, respecting the wreck :

> " I have with such provision in mine art
> So safely ordered, that there is no soul —
> No, nor so much perdition as an hair,
> Betid to any creature in the vessel —
> Which thou heard'st cry, which thou saw'st sink."
>
> Act i. Sc. 2.

> " All, but mariners,
> Plung'd in the foaming brine, and quit the vessel.
> Not a hair perish'd." Act i. Sc. 2.

> " But for the miracle,
> I mean our preservation."   Act ii. Sc. 1.

" There shall not a hair fall from the head of any of you."
Bible, Acts xxvii. 34.

" We were in all in the ship, two hundred threescore and sixteen souls."   ver. 37.

In the conversation between Prospero and Miranda, respecting their preservation in the "rotten carcass of a boat," in which they had been turn'd adrift, she asks:

> " How came we ashore ? "

He answers:

> " By Providence divine."

The Bible says :

" The centurion commanded that they which could swim should cast themselves first into the sea, and get to land : And the rest, some on boards, and some on broken pieces of the ship. And so it came to pass, that they escaped all safe to land."
Acts xxvii. 43, 44.

The sacred historian proceeds to inform us· that the barbarous people showed them no little kindness.

" And when Paul had gathered a bundle of sticks, and laid them on the fire, there came a viper out of the heat, and fastened on his hand. And when the barbarians saw the venomous beast hang on his hand, they said among themselves, no doubt this man is a murderer, whom, though he hath escaped the sea, yet vengeance suffereth not to live. And he shook off the beast into the fire, and felt no harm. Howbeit they looked when he should have swollen, or fallen down dead suddenly ; but after they had looked a great while, and saw no harm come to him, they changed their minds, and said that he was a god."
Acts xxviii. 2–6.

Shakespeare says of the people of the island :

> " Though they are of monstrous shape,
>   Their manners are more gentle, kind, than of
>   Our human generation you shall find
>   Many, nay almost any."   Act iii. Sc. 3.

" In the same quarters were possessions of the chief man of the island, whose name was Publius; who received us, and lodged us three days courteously. . . . . Who also honored us with many honors ; and when we departed, they laded us with such things as were necessary."   *Acts* xxviii. 7–10.

Shakespeare has also preserved the idea of gathering sticks.   Caliban says:

> " I 'll bear him no more sticks."   Act ii. Sc. 2.

And Ferdinand (Act ii. Scene 1) is introduced bearing a log.   Caliban talks of adders, Act iii. Scene 2.

" They changed their minds, and said that he was a god."
>   *Acts* xxviii. 2–6.

> " These be fine things, an' if they be not sprights.
>   That 's a brave god, etc."   Act ii. Sc. 11.

Prospero is represented as an old man, with a long beard, wearing a mantle, which is endowed with supernatural power.

> " Lend thy hand,
> And pluck my magic garment from me.— So.
>   [*Lays down his mantle.*]
> Lie there my art."   Act i. Sc. 11.

The idea of the "magic mantle" is no doubt borrowed from 1 Kings xix. and 2 Kings ii. 8: "And Elijah took his mantle, and smote the waters, and they were divided hither and thither, so that they too went over on dry ground."

He has also a rod, Act i. Scene 2 — Act v. Scene 1, with which he performs miracles, and controls the waters, which is, undoubtedly, taken from Moses; for besides the general idea, there are passages which incontestably show that he had the history of the Israelites in the wilderness in his mind; namely, that of the miraculous preservation of their garments.

"Thy raiment waxed not old upon thee, neither did thy foot swell, these forty years."   *Deut.* viii. 4.

"Yea, forty years, didst thou sustain them in the wilderness, so that they lacked nothing; their clothes waxed not old, and their feet swelled not."   *Nehemiah* ix. 21.

"On their sustaining garments not a blemish,
But fresher than before."   Act i. Sc. 2.

Though the island seems to be a *desert — uninhabitable* and almost *inaccessible* — yet it must needs be of a subtile, tender, and delicate temperature.

"Here is everything *advantageous to life*, but the rarity of it is, that our garments, being as they were drenched in the sea, hold notwithstanding their freshness and glosses, being rather new dy'd than stain'd with salt water."   Act ii. Sc. 1.

"Methinks our garments are now as fresh as when we put them on in Afric," etc.   Act ii. Sc. 1.

4

" Sir, we were talking that our garments seem now as fresh
as when we were at Tunis," etc.   Act ii. Sc. 1.

The name of Ariel is taken from Isaiah xxix. 1,
and Ezra viii. 16, and is a personification of air, as
Caliban is of earth. Ariel is thus described in the
Bible :

" And thou shalt be *brought down*, and thou shalt speak out
of the ground, and thy speech shall be low out of the dust, and
thy voice shall be as one that hath a *familiar spirit* out of the
ground; and thy speech shall whisper," etc. *Isaiah* xxix. 4.

The name of Ariel, used in Isaiah xxix. 1, applies
to the city of Jerusalem — " Wo to Ariel, the *city*
where David dwelt ! "

Shakespeare uses it as a spirit of air, gifting it with
the powers of his nature as a spirit — " his qualifica-
tion in sprighting."

Shakespeare evidently took the name of Ariel from
the Bible — not because its literal meaning was " the
Lion of God," but because it was a typical display
of divine justice, and, as such, Prospero uses this
"familiar spirit" for exactly the same purpose.

The play of " The Tempest " is an allegorical sketch,
intended to carry out a fanciful, if not a poetical idea
of the bard's, and certain ideas he may have formed
of men and manners. The zephyr-like Ariel, the image
of poetry, the dull, heavy, plodding, beastly Caliban,
the signification of earth — *earthly*. That portions of
the story may have been taken from other sources, we
have already shown, but that does not deprive the

Bible from its share in furnishing materials for it.
Even that beautiful passage:

> " And like the baseless fabric of this vision,
> The cloud-capp'd towers, the gorgeous palaces,
> The solemn temples, the great globe itself,
> Yea, all which it inherit, shall dissolve,
> And, like this unsubstantial pageant faded,
> Leave not a rack behind,"

finds its parallel in Scripture: — 1 Cor. vii. 31, " The
fashion of this world shall pass away,"

2 Peter iii. 10.   And the very " heavens shall pass
away with a great noise, and the elements shall melt
with fervent heat," when " the earth also, and the
works that are therein, shall be burnt up."

" All these things shall be dissolved."   V. II. 14.

"And the heavens departed as a scroll when it is rolled together, and every mountain and valley were moved out of their
places, ... For the great day of his wrath is come, and who
shall be able to stand ? "   *Revelation* vi. 14, 17.

Caliban says :

> " I 'll yield him thee asleep,
> Where thou may'st knock a nail into his head."
>
> Act iii. Sc. 11.

" Then Jael, Heber's wife, took a nail of the tent, and took a
hammer in her hand, and went softly unto him, and smote the
nail into his temples, and fastened it into the ground: for he was
fast asleep and weary.   So he died.

" And, behold, as Barak pursued Sisera, Jael came out to meet
him, and said unto him, Come, and I will show thee the man
whom thou seekest.   And when he came into her tent, behold
Sisera lay dead, and the nail was in his temples."

Judges iv. 21, 22.

Shakespeare unquestionably derived the idea of "The Tempest" from an early drama, not now known to exist, but of which a German version is preserved in Ayres's play, entitled "*Die Schöne Sidea*" (The Beautiful Sidea). As a proof of the fact, we annex the following points of resemblance : In the German drama, Prince Ludolph and Prince Leudegast supply the place of Prospero and Alonzo. Ludolph, like Prospero, is a magician, and like him has an only daughter, Sidea — the Miranda of the Tempest — and an attendant spirit, Runcifal, who, though not strictly resembling either Ariel or Caliban, may well be considered as the primary type which suggested to the poetic fancy of Shakespeare these strongly, yet admirably, contrasted beings. Shortly after the commencement of the play, Ludolph having been vanquished by his rival, and with his daughter Sidea driven into a forest, rebukes her for complaining of their change of fortune ; and then summons his spirit, Runcifal, to learn from him their future destiny and prospects of revenge. Runcifal, who is, like Ariel, somewhat moody, announces to Ludolph that the son of his enemy will shortly become his prisoner. After a comic episode, we see Prince Leudegast, with his son Engelbrecht and his companion Famulus, and the councillors, hunting in the same forest ; when Engelbrecht and his companion, Famulus, being separated from their associates, are suddenly encountered by Ludolph and his daughter. He commands them to yield themselves prisoners; they refuse, and try to draw their swords, when, as Prospero tells Ferdinand,

> " I can disarm thee with this stick,
> And make thy weapon drop —"

so Ludolph, with his wand, keeps their swords in
their scabbards, paralyzes Engelbrecht, and makes
him confess his

> " Nerves are in their infancy again,
> And have no vigor in them."

And when he has done so, gives him over as a slave
to Sidea, to carry logs for her. The resemblance
between this scene and the parallel scene in " The
Tempest," is rendered still more striking, when Sidea,
moved by pity for the labors of Engelbrecht, in carry-
ing logs, declares to him : " I am your wife, if you
will marry me,"— an event which, in the end, is
happily brought about, and leads to the reconciliation
of their parents, the rival princes.

We have shown that St. Paul's shipwreck on the
island of Melita furnished Shakespeare with the
materials for the supernatural characteristics of his
play, investing Prospero with an attribute, that Divine
power gave to the Apostle. It is somewhat surprising to us that Chalmers, Mrs. Jameson, Hunter,
Malone, and others, these " Old Mortalities," after
proof of the origin of " The Tempest," should have
skipped from shipwreck to shipwreck, from isle to
isle, from the " still vex'd Bermoothes" to the island
of Lampedusa, and left out that of Melita in the pur-
suit. To this, however, there can be no very especial

4 *

objection, although any other island, real or imaginary, in the Mediterranean or the Atlantic, would have answered as well. But there is not to be found in any romance or play, prior to the production of "The Tempest," a more remarkable identification with Scripture than that contained in this play, and which no other writer but a Shakespeare could have so reverently, and so admirably, blended with St. Paul's shipwreck on the island of Melita.

Hazlett, the accomplished lecturer on dramatic literature, speaking of "The Tempest," says : "The Tempest is one of the most original and perfect of Shakespeare's productions, and he has shown in it all the variety of his powers. It is full of grace and grandeur. The human and imaginary characters, the dramatic and the grotesque, are blended together with the greatest art, and without any appearance of it. Though he has given ' to airy nothing a local habitation and a name,' yet that part which is only the fantastic creation of his mind, has the same palpable texture, and coheres ' sensibly with the rest.' "

In Othello, there are numerous passages of scriptural familiarity, and what is more remarkable, Shakespeare seems to have adopted the peculiar style of the inspired Apostles. For instance, in Othello, Æmelia introduces the following, which contains a direct reference to Scripture :

> " If any wretch hath put this in your head,
>   Let Heaven requite it with the serpent's curse."
>
> Act iv. Sc. 2.

Othello says: "Rude am I in speech." In 2 Corinthians xv. 6, we read, "But though I am rude in speech," etc. Also the Moor uses the following :

> "I took by the throat the circumcised dog,
> And smote him — thus."

In 1 Samuel xvii. 35, we have the following :

"I smote him, I caught him by his beard, and smote him, and slew him."

Othello says: "Haply, for I am black;" also in the "Merchant of Venice," we have the same in a somewhat different form :

> "Mislike me not for my complexion,
> The shadow'd livery of the burning sun."
> > Act ii. Sc. 1.

"Look not upon me because I am black, because the sun hath looked upon me." *Solomon's Songs* i. 6.

Othello, in his speech commencing with, "Had it pleased heaven to try me with affliction, had it rained all kinds of sores and shame on my bare head, etc.," is not unlike this passage in Job ii. 6–8.

"So, went Satan forth from the presence of the Lord, and smote Job with sore boils from the sole of his foot unto his crown, etc."

In the following beautiful passages we have the happiest assurance of Shakespeare's veneration for our blessed Saviour.

" Over whose acres walked those blessed feet,
    Which fourteen hundred years ago were nailed
    For our advantage on the bitter cross."

Henry IV., Act i. Sc. 1.

" But when your carters, or your waiting vassals,
    Have done a drunken slaughter, and defaced
    The image of our Redeemer, etc."

Richard III., Act ii. Sc. 1.

" Like a drunken sailor on a mast."

Richard III., Act iii. Sc. 4.

This passage is evidently taken from *Proverbs* xxiii. 34 :

" He lieth on the top of a mast."

" I die daily."   1 *Cor.* xv. 31.

" Thy royal father
Was a most sainted King; the Queen that bore thee,
Oftener upon her knees than on her feet,
Died every day she lived."   *Macbeth*, Act iv. Sc. 3.

" And the man of thine, whom I shall not cut off from mine altar, shall be to consume thine eyes, and to grieve thine heart."   1 *Samuel* ii. 33.

" Show his eyes, and grieve her heart."

Macbeth, Act iv. Sc. 1.

Macbeth says :

" Lighted fools the way to dusty death."

In the Psalms we find the following :

" Thou hast brought me unto the dust of death."

Dusty death alludes to the sentence pronounced against Adam :

> " Dust thou art, and unto dust thou shalt return."
>
> *Gen.* iii. 19.

> " May this accursed hour stand, aye
> Accursed in thy calendar."
>
> *Macbeth*, Act iv. Sc. 1.

" After that night let darkness seize upon it — let it not be found unto the days of the year — let it not come into the number of the months, . . . Let them curse it that curse the day." *Job* iii. 6–8.

> " We will die with harness on our back."
>
> *Macbeth*, Act v. Sc. 5.

> " Nicanor lay dead in his harness."
>
> 2 *Maccabees* xv. 20.

> *Banquo.*— " Fears and scruples shake us ;
> In the great hand of God I stand, and thence
> Against the undivulged pretense I fight
> Of treasonable malice." *Macbeth*, Act ii. Sc. 3.

" Thou hast also given me the shield of thy salvation ; and thy right hand hath holden me up." *Ps.* xviii. 35.

Hermia and Lear both use an expression derived from the same source :

> *Hermia.*— " An adder did it, for with doubler tongue
> Than thine, thou serpent, never adder stung."
>
> *Midsummer-Night's Dream*, Act iii. Sc. 2.

> *Lear.*— " Struck me with her tongue,
> Most serpent-like, upon the very heart."
>
> Act ii. Sc. 4.

"They have sharpened their tongues like a serpent's; adder's poison is under their lips." *Ps.* cxi. 3.

Lear. — "All the stored vengeance of heaven fall on her ungrateful top." Act ii. Sc. 4.

"As for the head of those that compass me about; let the mischief of their own lips cover them." *Ps.* cxi. 9.

Fool to King Lear.— "We'll send thee to school to an ant, to teach thee there's no laboring in winter." Act ii. Sc. 4.

"The ants are a people not strong; yea, they prepare their meat in summer." *Prov.* xxx. 25; also *Prov.* vi. 6.

"Or memorize another Golgotha."
Macbeth, Act i. Sc. 2.

"And they bring him unto a place, Golgotha, which being interpreted — the place of a skull." *Mark* xv. 22.

"Against the Lord's anointed." *Richard III.*

"For who can stretch forth his hand against the Lord's anointed?" 1 *Samuel* xxvi. 9.

"Life's but a walking shadow." *Shakespeare.*

"Man walketh in a vain shadow." *Bible.*

"In his true nature; and we ourselves compelled,
   Even to the teeth and forehead of our faults,
      To give in evidence." *Hamlet*, Act iii. Sc. 3.

"At that time, Jesus answered and said: I thank thee, O Father, Lord of heaven and earth, because thou hast hid these things from the wise and prudent, and hast revealed them unto babes." *Matthew* xi. 25.

"He, that of greatest works is finished,
   Oft does them by the weakest means,

> So holy writ in babies hath judgment shown,
> When judges have been babies."
> > *All's Well that Ends Well*, Act ii. Sc. 2.

" A man's heart deviseth his way; but the Lord directeth his steps." *Prov.* xvi. 9.

> " There's a divinity that shapes our ends,
> Roughhew them as you will."
> > *Hamlet*, Act v. Sc. 2.

" What a piece of work is man — how noble in reason, how infinite in faculties; in form and moving, how express and admirable; in action, how like an angel; in apprehension, how like a god." *Hamlet*, Act ii. Sc. 2.

" What is man, that thou art mindful of him? and the son of man, that thou visitest him?

" For thou hast made him a little lower than the angels, and hast crowned him with glory and honor.

" Thou mad'st him to have dominion over the works of thy hands; thou hast put all things under his feet."

> *Ps.* viii. 4-6.

This beautiful passage from the Psalms, afforded Shakespeare and Dr. Young an opportunity of inditing two of the most sublime apostrophes to man that are to be found in the English language. In many of the most striking allusions Shakespeare makes to the Bible — at times borrowing, as we have shown, whole passages— he not only displays the most intimate knowledge of the text, but an insight into what superficial readers might call " mysteries." His illustrations of the Bible are equally potent, and how admirably he adapts scriptural incidents to those of his plays. It will also be observed that Shakespeare selects out the highest and most sublime passages of the Bible, as well as ideas, for his dramatic illustrations. For instance, he compares good to light, because God created light, and pronounced it good. He also compares evil to darkness, illustrating the latter in that terrible passage in Macbeth:

> " Come, thick night,
> And pall thee in the dunnest smoke of hell!
> That my keen knife see not the wound it makes,
> Nor heaven peep through the blanket of the dark,
> To cry, ' Hold, hold.' " *Macbeth,* Act i. Sc. 6.

Again, how apt the use of scriptural parables. Nathan's parable, which was designed " to catch the conscience of the king " (Hamlet, Act ii.), was a fictitious story, something like the circumstances of David's case, in the murder of Uriah, intended to excite his attention, and make him pass judgment upon himself in the character of the rich man (2 Samuel xii.), and which Shakespeare uses, making it one of the most effective scenes in this great play, to " catch the conscience of the king."

In the " Merchant of Venice," the poet makes use of the history of Jacob and Laban, which Bishop Wadsworth cites " as a remarkable instance of the tact which Shakespeare could apply with perfect accuracy a passage of Scripture open to misconception, and yet divest its application of all dangerous tendency." This passage concludes with the following:

" The devil can quote Scripture to his purpose.
   An evil soul, producing holy witness,
   Is like a villain with a smiling cheek:
   A goodly apple, rotten at the heart;
   O, what a goodly outside falsehood hath."

Act i. Sc. 3.

Bishop Wadsworth, speaking of this line, " The devil can quote Scripture," etc., says : There is evidently an allusion to the history of our Lord's temptation, as recorded in Matthew iv. and Luke iv., and the same allusion occurs again in Richard III., where the wicked Gloster is speaking of the treason and other crimes which he had committed, and not only discussed, but laid to the charge of others, who, he pretended, had by those same crimes wronged and displeased him.

" But then I sigh, and with a piece of Scripture
   Tell them, that God bids us do good for evil:
   And thus I clothe my naked villany
   With odd old ends stol'n forth of holy writ,
   And seem a saint, when most I play the devil."

Richard III., Act i. Sc. 3.

The " Merchant of Venice " is one of Shakespeare's most perfect works. The whole of it abounds with scriptural allusions, many of which are introduced most admirably by the great master-spirit of the " mimic world," to carry out the design of the plot and illustrate the peculiar characteristics of his *dramatis personæ*. The student of divinity can read the

5   D

"Merchant of Venice," and find therein much instruction, blended with amusement.

What, in the English language, more beautifully describes night than that exquisite night scene in the play, Act v. Scene 1, commencing, "The moon shines bright : — In such a night as this," etc.? The beauty and truthfulness of this description is only equalled by the poetic garb in which the author clothes it.

A writer, speaking of it, says : "It is the intense feeling of reality in this scene that, to my mind, gives strong confirmation of the opinion that Shakespeare had, at some period prior to the drama, wandered beneath the skies and moons of Italy." We give the closing passage of this sublime apostrophe to night :

> " How sweet the moonlight sleeps upon the bank !
> Here we will sit, and let the sounds of music
> Creep in our ears ; soft stillness, and the night,
> Become the touches of sweet harmony.
> Sit, Jessica : Look how the floor of heaven
> Is thick inlaid with patens of bright gold."

Shakespeare's allusions to music are more or less based on those contained in the Bible ; he invariably speaks of it as "holy music revealing to the soul of men a past which they never have known, and futurity, which in this life they never can know."

The language of the Holy Scriptures breathes throughout that peculiar tone which vibrates upon the heart and teaches us that music came in with the creation, in one pure strain of harmony. David, the Psalm-

ist, stands before us the minstrel of Jehovah, the harper
of his time, whose songs were an epitome of the sacred
writings, adapted to the purposes of religion. Nor is
it surprising that his beautiful illustrations shadowed
forth the coming of our Saviour in all the bright imagery of poetic beauty. In the early history and formation of the world, Deity conducted the vast orches-
tra which sent forth the music of creation to harmon-
ize with the works of His hand — not a note or a sound
but what was scaled by Him ; even the planets moved
to the strains of heavenly music, and Shakespeare, the
creator of the " mimic world," thus beautifully alludes
to the music of the spheres :

> " There is not the smallest orb which thou behold'st
> But in his motion like an angel sings."

Shakespeare evidently derived the idea of the orbs
being musical from the philosophical imagination of
Plato, who, in his " Republic " and " Timocus,"
nearly two thousand years before Shakespeare, had
taught that the heavenly bodies in their revolutions
produced, by their rapid motion, the most exquisite
musical harmony. This idea is in some measure sanc-
tioned by Proclus, who asserts that even "the growth
of plants is attended with sound." Connected with the
simple plant wild mandrake (*Podophyllum*), is the following beautiful allegorical legend — we say allegorical, although the very formation of the simple plant
gives it the means of producing sounds, which its
botanical classification explains. It is said to breathe

fo th, at certain times, the most plaintive sounds and melancholy moans, indicative of pain or suffering. It is also said to utter, as it were, a wild scream or shriek, if rudely torn from its bed! We mention this merely for its poetic legendary character, as we possess no actual proof of its foundation in truth.

We now turn to a less refined character of the bard's creation, Sir John Falstaff. "This," says Hazlett, "is perhaps the most substantial comic character that ever was invented." We think Shakespeare erred in putting scriptural phrases into the mouth of this gross lump of fat. Many of these phrases are irreverent, although characteristic of the man. Falstaff is a peculiar character; in him "we behold the fulness of the spirit of wit and humor bodily." His very grossness becomes refined beneath the touch of the poet, and his jokes come upon us with double force and relish from the quantity of flesh through which they make their way, as he shakes his fat sides with laughter, or "lards the lean earth as he walks along." These passages from Scripture come from him with a gusto that makes us forget their source: "Pitch doth defile," "The tree is known by its fruit," "Pharaoh's lean kine," "Hues that lived in purple," "Adam fell," "Ragged as Lazarus," etc.

Let us give another illustration from Hamlet showing still more how closely the bard had studied Holy Writ, and how aptly he introduces striking passages to answer his purpose:

" Look here upon this picture, and on this —
The counterfeit presentment of two brothers.
See, what a grace was seated on this brow :
Hyperion's curls; the front of Jove himself;
An eye like Mars, to threaten and command;
A station like the herald Mercury,
New-lighted on a heaven-kissing hill :
A combination, and a form, indeed,
Where every god did seem to set his seal,
To give the world assurance of a man.
This was your husband. —
Look you, now, what follows :
Here is your husband ; *like a mildew'd ear,
Blasting his wholesome brother."*

Hamlet, Act iii. Sc. 4.

" And I saw in my dream, and behold, seven ears came up
in one stalk, full and good.

" And behold, seven ears, withered, thin, and blasted with
the east wind, sprang up after them.

" And the thin ears devoured the seven good ears."

Gen. xli. 22, 23, 24.

" Masters, spread yourselves."
Midsummer-Night's Dream, Act i. Sc. 2.

"Spreading himself like a green bay-tree."   *Ps.* xxxvii. 35.

" Swear by thy gracious self."

Romeo and Juliet.

" He could not swear by no greater, he swore by himself."
Heb. vi. 13.

" Wilt thou set thy foot o' my neck ? "
Twelfth Night, Act ii. Sc. 5.

" And they came near and put their feet upon the necks of
them."   *Josh.* x. 24.

5 *

"Who can call him friend, that dips in the same dish."
Timon of Athens.

" And he answered and said, he that dippeth the hand with me in the same dish, the same shall betray me."   *The Bible.*

"It is written they appear to men like angels of light."
Comedy of Errors.

"Satan himself is transformed into an angel of light."
2 Cor. xi. 14.

"Besides, the king's name is a tower of strength."
Richard III., Act v. Sc. 3.

"The name of the Lord is a strong tower."
Prov. xviii. 10.

In "Antony and Cleopatra," we have a reference to the bulls of Bashan :

"Oh, that I were
Upon the hill of Bashan to outroar
The horned herd, for I have a savage cause,
And to proclaim it civilly, were like
A halted neck, which does the hangman thank, etc."

In Richard III., at the end of Act i., the second murderer of Clarence says :

"How fain, like Pilate, would I wash my hands
Of this most grievous guilty murder done."

Readers familiar with the New Testament can readily trace its source, as also the following :

"Consideration like an angel came,
And whipp'd the offending Adam out of him ;

Leaving his body as a paradise,
To envelope and contain celestial spirits."

Henry V., Act i. Sc. 1.*

" He that doth the ravens feed,
Yea, providently caters for the sparrow, etc."

As You Like It, Act ii. Sc. 3.

" Are not two sparrows sold for a farthing? and one of them shall not fall on the ground without your father.

" The very hairs of your head are all numbered."

Matt. x. 29, 30.

" Behold the fowls of the air; for they sow not, neither do they reap, nor gather into barns; yet your heavenly Father feedeth them."   *Matt.* vi. 26.

In the last scene of Richard III. there is mention made of the holy sacrament. After the battle, Richmond says:

" Proclaim a pardon to the soldiers fled,
That in submission will return to us;
And thus as we have ta'en the sacrament
We will unite the White rose with the Red."

" Woe to that land, that's govern'd by a child."

Richard III., Act ii. Sc. 2.

" Woe to thee, O land, when the king is a child." .

Eccl. x. 16.

" Man is the image of his own Maker."

Henry VII.

---

* Bishop Stome, in his sermon on " The Duty of taking up the Cross," in alluding to this passage from Shakespeare, says : " Does the father hate his child whom he chastises ? No, it is the best proof he can show of his love. So saith our Heavenly Father of His children. Whom the Lord loveth he chasteneth, and scourgeth every son whom he receiveth."

" So God created man in His own image."   *Gen.* i. 27.

" That which you speak, is in your own conscience, washed as pure as sin with baptism."   *King Henry.*

" Be baptized and wash away thy sins."   *Acts* xxii. 16.

" I told ye all,
When we first put this dangerous stone a rolling, 't would fall upon ourselves."   *Henry VIII.*, Sc. 2.

" He that rolleth a stone, it will return upon him."
Proverbs xxvi. 27.

We consider the following expression highly irreverent, more particularly as it has been incorporated in the slang language of the day :

" Could I come near your beauty with my nails,
I 'd set my ten commandments in your face." *
2 *King Henry VI.*, Act i. Sc. 3.

" Blessed are the peacemakers on earth,"
Henry VII., Act iii. Sc. 1.

is taken literally from Matthew.

" My stay, my guide, and lantern to my feet."   Act iii. Sc. 3.

---

* This phrase would seem more fitting in the mouth of a fish-woman than that of a lady. It was, however, a common expression used by dramatists before Shakespeare's time. Thus in the " Four P's," 1569 :

" Now ten times I beseech him that hie sits
Thy wife's X Com. may search thy five wits."

And in " Westward Hoe," 1607 : " Your harpy has set his ten commandments on my back."

"Thy word is a lamp unto my feet, and a light unto my path."
Psalms cxix. 105.

"Like sacrificing Abel's cries,
E'en from the tongueless caverns of the earth."
Richard III.

"What hast thou done? the voice of thy brother's blood crieth unto me from the ground. And now art thou accursed from the earth, which hath opened her mouth to receive thy brother's blood from thy hand." *Genesis* iv. 10, 11.

"And when he falls, he falls like Lucifer."
Henry VIII., Act iii. Sc. 2.

Manifestly borrowed from that fine passage in Isaiah xiv. 12 :

"How art thou fallen from Heaven, O Lucifer, son of the morning."

"No, Bolingbroke, if ever I were a traitor,
My name be blotted from the book of life."

Evidently taken from this passage in Revelation :

"Whose names were not written in the book of life."

Shakespeare is also indebted to Holy Writ for this passage, introduced in that great soliloquy of Richard II., Act v. Scene 5, commencing with

"I have been studying how I may compare
This prison, where I live, unto the world."

During which he introduces the following :

"As thus, come, little ones,"
and then again :

> " It is hard to come, as for a camel
> To thread the postern of a needle's eye."

Shakespeare evidently had the following passages in his mind when he wrote King Richard's soliloquy :

" It is easier for a camel to go through the eye of a needle, than for a rich man to enter the kingdom of God."

" Suffer little children, and forbid them not, to come unto me, for of such is the kingdom of Heaven."   *Matthew* xix. 14.

> " The quality of mercy is not strained;
> It droppeth, as the gentle rain from heaven,
> Upon the place beneath; it is twice blessed;
> It blesses him that gives, and him that takes."
> > *Merchant of Venice,* Act iv. Sc. 1.

" As the dew that descendeth upon the mountains of Zion."
> *Psalm* cxxxiii. 3.

The Scriptures abound with instances of the mercy of God, nor was it likely Shakespeare would pass the word over. How beautifully he has described this Divine attribute, the above passage shows. He who, in his great commands, is so unlimited in this virtue, and says he will " Show mercy unto thousands of those who love me, and keep my commandments," will not forget those who practise it here. *Exodus* xx. 6.

" And lose my way among the thorns and dangers of the world."
> *King John.*

> " Thorns and snares are in the way of the froward."
> > *Proverbs* xxii. 5.

In "Troilus and Cressida," Act i. Scene 3, the speech of Ulysses is almost a paraphrase of the twenty-first chapter of St. Luke. It commences:

> " But when the planets
> In evil mixture, to disorder wander,
> What plagues, and what portents? What mutiny?
> What raging of the sea? shaking of earth?
> Commotions of the winds? fights, changes, horrors,
> Shrink and crack, rend and deracinate
> The unity and married calm of states,
> Quite from their mixture?"

Quotation from Luke:

" And there shall be signs in the sun, and in the moon, and in the stars, and upon the earth distress of nations, with perplexity: the sea and the waves roaring; men's hearts failing them from fear, and for looking after those things which are coming on earth; for the powers of heaven shall be shaken."

That the most sublime doctrines of our holy religion may be introduced on the stage, if done with seriousness and address, the following passage will show.

In "Measure for Measure," in the scene where Isabella is pleading with Angelo for her brother's life, he says:

> " Your brother is a forfeit of the law,
> And you but waste words.
> *Isabella.—* Alas! alas!
> Why all the souls that were, were forfeit once,
> And He that might the 'vantage best have took,

> Found out the remedy. How would you be,
> If He, which is the top of judgment, should
> But judge you as you are? Oh, think on that,
> And mercy then will breathe within your lips
> Like man made new."   Act ii. Sc. 2.

At the conclusion of the speech of Portia, in "The Merchant of Venice," on the attribute of mercy, she says:

> "Therefore, Jew,
> Though justice be thy plea, consider this:
> That in the course of justice, none of us
> Should see salvation: we do pray for mercy;
> And that same prayer doth teach us all to render
> The deeds of mercy."   Act iv. Sc. 1.

In Hamlet, Act i. Scene 1, we find this beautiful passage:

> "Some say, that ever 'gainst that season comes
> Wherein our Saviour's birth is celebrated,
> The bird of dawning singeth all night long;
> And then they say no spirit can walk abroad;
> No fairy takes, nor witch hath power to charm,
> So hallow'd and so gracious is the time."

The idea of fairies and witches having power at night seems to have been a popular superstition. Imogen, in "Cymbeline," when she is in bed and about to go to sleep, says:

> "To your protection I commend me, gods!
> From fairies, and the tempters of the night,
> Guard me, beseech you."   Act ii. Sc. 2.

Here the prayer is addressed to the wrong object, and admits the existence of fairies.

As instances of bad characters, vices, etc., introduced with their antidotes, we will mention Macbeth and his lady, and Falstaff, in the second part of Henry IV.

The compunctious visiting of Macbeth during the time he is meditating the murder, his reflections afterwards, and the remorse of his guilty conscience, are fine and instructive. So are the following reflections of Lady Macbeth, even at the first entrance upon their wickedly acquired state:

> " Nought's bad, all's spent,
>   When our desire is got without content;
>   'Tis safer to be that which we destroy,
>   Than, by destruction, dwell in doubtful joy."
>   Act iii. Sc. 2.

And the scene where she is represented walking in her sleep, rehearsing the dreadful scene of the murder of Duncan, disclosing the secret of her guilty soul, is another valuable lesson. So, likewise, are the reflections of Macbeth, Act v. Scene 3:

> "I have liv'd long enough; my May of life
>   Is fall'n into the sear, the yellow leaf;
>   And that which should accompany old age,
>   As honor, love, obedience, troops of friends,
>   I must not look to have; but in their stead,
>   Curses not loud, but deep, mouth-honor, breath
>   Which the poor heart would fain deny, but dare not."

6

The disgrace of Sir John Falstaff, at the end of the second part of Henry IV., is good. When Falstaff presents himself to his old companion, the Prince, then just crowned Henry V., the king says to him:

> "I know thee not, old man: Fall to thy prayers;
> How ill white hairs become a fool and jester!
> I have long dream'd of such a kind of man,
> So surfeit swell'd, so old, and so profane;
> But, being awake, I do despise my dream.
> Make less thy body, hence, and more thy grace;
> Leave gormandizing; know thy grave doth gape
> For thee thrice wider than for other men."
>
> Act v. Sc. 5.

This, we think, however, comes with a very ill grace from one who had scarcely divested himself of the habits acquired from the one whom he now so summarily dismissed from his presence. It is very much like Satan reproving sin. Dr. Johnson, in a note at the end of the play, says: "The moral to be drawn from this representation, is, that no man is more dangerous than he that, with a will to corrupt, hath the power to please, and that neither wit nor honesty ought to think themselves safe with such a companion, when they see Henry seduced by Falstaff."

> "Though some of you, with Pilate, wash your hands,
> Showing an outward pity; yet you Pilates
> Have here deliver'd me to my sour cross,
> And water cannot wash away your sin."
>
> *King Richard II.*, Act iv. Sc. 1.

"When Pilate saw that he could prevail nothing, but rather a tumult was made, he took water, and washed his hands before the multitude, saying, I am innocent of the blood of this just person."   *Matthew* xxvii. 24.

There are other passages in this great play of a decidedly scriptural character, as for instance:

> "Yet, I well remember
> The favors of these men: were they not mine?
> Did they not sometimes cry, All hail! to me?
> So Judas did to Christ; but he, in twelve,
> Found truth in all but one: I, in twelve thousand, none."
>   *Richard II.*, Act iv. Sc. 1.

"Now he that betrayed him gave them a sign, saying, 'Whomsoever I shall kiss, that same is he;— hold him fast.'

"And forthwith he came to Jesus, and said, 'Hail, Master,' and kissed him."   *Matthew* xxvi. 48, 49.

Shakespeare, whenever he introduces a character that has all the attributes of evil in his nature, seems to have some one always in his "mind's eye" as an illustration. If profane history does not furnish him with the object, he is sure to find one in the Bible, and in Judas, the character is peculiarly adapted to answer his purpose, when putting words into the mouth of the treacherous Richard (III.), in King Henry, Act v. Scene 7, where he hypocritically greets the king, who is discovered on his throne, with Queen Elizabeth, the infant Prince, Clarence, Gloster, Hastings, and others near him. Gloster, after professing affection for the infant, and receiving the thanks of the king, says:

"And, that
I love the tree from whence thou sprang'st,
Witness the loving kiss I give thee first."

(*Aside.*) "To say the truth, so Judas kiss'd his master,
And cried, All hail! Whence as he meant all harm."

"Abraham went with them to bring them on their way."
Genesis xviii. 16.

"I pray you, bring me on the way a little."
Othello, Act iii. Sc. 4.

"This people draweth nigh unto me with their mouth, and
honoreth me with their lips; but their heart is far from me."
Matthew xv. 8.

"When I would pray and think, I think and pray
To several subjects, Heaven hath my empty words;
Whilst my invention, hearing not my tongue,
Anchors on Isabel : Heaven in my mouth,
And if I did but only chew His name;
And in my heart, the strong and swelling evil
Of my conception."
Measure for Measure, Act ii. Sc. 4.

"For God shall bring every work into judgment, with every
secret thing, whether it be good, or whether it be evil."
Eccl. xii. 14.

"But 't is not so above;
There, is no shuffling; there, the action lies
In his true nature; and we ourselves compell'd,
Even to the teeth and forehead of our faults,
To give in evidence."   *Hamlet,* Act iii. Sc. 3.

Shakespeare in many instances followed the scriptural manner of writing, as, for instance:

"Our Father *which* art in heaven." Again, in Gen. xviii. 27 : "Behold, now, I have taken upon me to speak unto the Lord, *which* am but dust and ashes." In Matt. xxvii. 55, 56, we have "which" for both "who" and "whom." "And many women were there beholding afar off, *which* followed Jesus," etc. Both usages are to be met in Shakespeare. Thus, in "The Tempest," Act iii. Sc. 1, Ferdinand says : "The mistress *which* I serve," and in King Richard III : "Those uncles *which* you want, were dangerous," etc. A writer speaking of Shakespeare's use of scriptural words, instead of those of his own, as more suited to the age in which he lived, says : "There is nothing which occurs to me, as calling for remark in connection with the grammar of adjectives, except the use of double comparatives and superlatives. Of the former, Shakespeare would seem to have been specially fond. I have noted more than thirty examples, and among them, '.more better,' also, 'worser' and ' more worse ' repeated several times. ' More richer,' ' more worthier,' ' more corrupter,' and 'more worse,' are all to be found in ' King Lear,' one of our poet's later and more finished productions."

The word Bravery, is used but once in the Bible :

"In that day the Lord will take away the bravery of their tinkling ornaments about their feet." *Isaiah* iii. 18.

Shakespeare uses it seven times, and in one instance he evidently had the above passage in his mind, for he says :

6 *   E

" With scarfs and fans and double change of bravery."
Taming of the Shrew, Act iv. Sc. 3.

The writer, alluded to, occupies in his little book forty-two pages, under the head of " Noticeable forms of speech in the English Bible found also in Shakespeare."

In the account of David's encounter with Goliath, it is said:

" The staff of whose spear was like a weaver's beam."
I *Sam.* xvii. 7.

Shakespeare uses in the "Merry Wives of Windsor," where Falstaff declares:

" In the shape of man, master Brook, I fear not Goliath with a weaver's beam, because I know also life is a shuttle."
Act v. Sc. 1.

" Thou art a traitor —
Off with his head! Now, by St. Paul, I swear,
I will not dine until I see the same."
Richard III., Act iii. Sc. 4.

" Certain of the Jews banded together, and bound themselves under a curse, saying that they would neither eat nor drink till they had killed Paul." *Acts* xxiii. 12.

Apart from Shakespeare's biblical knowledge, there is a much more important fact connected with it, and that is, he makes use of the Scripture as one who reverenced it, and entertained the idea of its being an inspiration of Deity, "revealing His general and particular Providence, His revelation to man, of our duty towards each other, of human life and of human death, of time and eternity; in a word, of every subject which it most concerns us, as rational and responsible beings, to conceive."

Throughout the works of Shakespeare he treats " of the Being and nature of God," with a degree of solemnity that no pulpit expounder has ever yet exceeded. Shakespeare speaks of Deity as the Divine Omniscience, one who knows all things, sees all things, even our most secret thoughts; that He neither slumbers nor sleeps, and that His ways are not as our ways. In "All 's Well that Ends Well," Act ii. Scene 1, is the illustration we wish to convey:

> " It is not so with Him that all things knows,
>   As 't is with us that square our guess by shows;
>   But most it is presumption in us, when
>   The help of Heaven we count the act of men."

" I will speak daggers."   *Hamlet*, Act iii. Sc. 2.

"Swords are in their lips."   *Psalm* lix. 7.

" Wisdom and goodness to the vile seem vile."
                              King Lear, Act iv. Sc. 2.

" Wo unto you when all men speak well of you."
                              Luke vi. 26.

> " Thy greatest help is quiet, gentle Nell;
>   I pray thee, sort thy heart to patience."
>   2 *King Henry VI.*, Act ii. Sc. 4.

" Their strength is to sit still. In quietness and in confidence shall be your strength."   *Isaiah* xxx. 7, 15.

" Pride must have a fall."   *Richard II.*, Act v. Sc. 5.

" Pride goeth before destruction, and a haughty spirit before a fall." *Proverbs* xvi. 18.

" And will not you maintain the thing you teach."
1 *King Henry VI.*, Act iii. Sc. 1.

" Thou, therefore, which teachest another, teachest thou not thyself." *Rom.* ii. 21.

Many passages in the plays of Shakespeare might be quoted to prove his religious sentiments ; others again, when putting words into the mouths of his characters, might also be given as an evidence of his unbelief. We must not take the isolated passages of an author as an evidence of his being a Christian, or an infidel. Byron's Cain has been so often quoted to prove him an atheist, that the reading public have become reconciled to the story, as the invention of weak minds, who are unable to distinguish the difference between the author and the characters he introduces. If Satan is essential to his story, Satan must talk as such a being necessarily would. The same with those who believe as he does, and act in conformity to his lessons.

The peace to which the spirits of good men are admitted immediately upon their dissolution, is twice mentioned by the poet under the figure by which we find it represented in the New Testament.

" And in hell he lifted up his eyes, being in torments, and seeth Abraham afar off, and Lazarus in his bosom."
Luke xvi. 23.

Here is mentioned, on the one hand, the torment

of bad men after death, as represented by parable, as also alluded to in Luke xxiii. 4, in reference to our Lord's promise to the penitent thief. (See King Henry VI., 2d part, Act v. Scene 1.)

The parallel passage in Shakespeare to that in Luke xvi. 23, is as follows: Bolingbroke, speaking of the death of Norfolk:

> " Is Norfolk dead ? "

Carlisle answers :

> " As sure as I live, my lord."

Bolingbroke.— " Sweet peace conduct his sweet soul to the bosom of good old Abraham ! "

> *King Richard II.*, Act iv. Sc. 1.

Richard III. has the same allusion, although uttered in a far different spirit :

> " The sons of Edward sleep in Abraham's bosom."
>> Act iv. Sc. 4.

In Macbeth, Act ii. Scene 3, there is an allusion to hell ; and, as a place of punishment, is spoken of as being perpetual :

> " I had thought to have let in some of all professions that go the primrose way to the *everlasting* bonfire."

A similar passage to this is found in " All's Well," Act iv. Scene 5.

> " I am for the house with the narrow gate, which I take to

be too little for pomp to enter; some that humble themselves may; but the many will be too chill and tender; and they'll be for the flowery way, *that leads to the broad gate and the great fire.*"

A learned writer, speaking of Shakespeare's sentiments derived from the Bible, says: "It was to be expected that the circumstances of the judgment day, as they are revealed to us in Scripture, would make a deep and lasting impression upon a mind like Shakespeare's. Accordingly, when he desires to give more than ordinary effect to deep passion, to indignation and abhorrence at crime committed, or to affliction and distress at calamity incurred, he has recourse to images which are associated with the final doom — the sounding of the last trump, the discomfiture of creation, the dissolution of the heavens and the earth. Thus, first in the concluding scene of King Lear, where the fact that the personages of the play are all Pagans, would not allow of more than a general and indistinct allusion to the 'promised end,' we read as follows: "

Lear.— " Howl — howl — howl — howl ! O, you are men of
        stones;
        Had I your tongues and eyes, I'd use them so
        That heaven's vault should crack.
    .   .   .   .   .

  Kent.— Is this the promised end ?
  Edgar.— Or image of that horror ? "

See Matthew xxiv. 6: " The end is not yet;" and Peter iv. 7: " The end of all things is at hand."

There is the same kind of indistinct reference to

the gospel record of our Lord's combined prophecy of the destruction of Jerusalem, and of the end of the world, in a speech of Gloster's towards the beginning of the same play:

"These late eclipses in the sun and moon portend no good to us; . . . . Love cools, friendship falls off, brothers divide; in cities, mutinies; in countries, discord; in palaces, treason; and the bond cracked between son and father. This villain of mine comes under the prediction: there's son against father; the king falls from bias of nature; there's father against child."
                                                    Act i. Sc. 2.

And now the curtain of our teacher drops on the great scene of the prophecies, and of revelations:

"We know not, even with the help of the latter, what the end, or what we shall be hereafter."

"Beloved, now are we the sons of God; and it doth not yet appear what we shall be."   I *John* iii. 2.

This idea is carried out in Hamlet:

"Lord, we know what we are, but know not what we may be."   Act iv. Sc. 5.

"The end is not yet," as the Bible foreshadows its coming, so does the great poet, but not until

> "The solemn temples, the great globe itself,
> Yea, all which it inherit, shall dissolve,
> And, like this insubstantial pageant faded,
> Leave not a rack behind."

It is evident, therefore, that of all the books which

Shakespeare studied in his own language, there was none with which he was more familiar than with the English Bible. Aureles, whom we have already quoted, says: " That in every instance the characters in his plays have treated Holy Scripture with the nice and exact reverence which we should feel to be desirable at the present day, is not to be maintained ; but still less is the charge which has been brought against him, of frequent irreverence, and profaneness in the use of God's word, to be justified and received."

> . . . " So soon we shall drive back
> Of Alcibiades th' approaches wild ;
> Who like a boar too savage, doth root up
> His country's peace."
>
> *Timon of Athens,* Act v. Sc. 2.

> " The boar out of the wood doth waste it,
> And the wild beast of the field doth devour it."
>
> *Ps.* lxxx. 13.

> " The throne he sits on, nor the tide of pomp
> That beats upon the high shore of this world;
> No, not all these, thrice gorgeous ceremony,
> Not all these laid in bed majestical,
> Can sleep so soundly as the wretched slave,
> Who, with a body filled, and vacant mind,
> Gets him to rest, cramm'd with distressful bread," etc.
>
> *King Henry V.,* Act iv. Sc. 1.

" The sleep of a laboring man is sweet, whether he eat little or much ; but the abundance of the rich will not suffer him to sleep."

> *Eccl.* v. 12.

> . . . " Weariness
> Can snore upon the flint, when restive sloth
> Finds the down pillow hard."
>
> *Cymbeline,* Act. iii. Sc. 6.

" And why beholdest thou the mote that is in thy brother's eye, but considerest not the beam that is in thine own eye."

Matthew vii. 3.

"You found his mote; the king your mote did see;
But I a beam do find in each eye of thee."

Love's Labor's Lost, Act iv. Sc. 3.

"Look not thou upon the wine when it is red, when it giveth his color in the cup, when it moveth itself aright. At the last it biteth like a serpent, and stingeth like an adder."

Prov. xxiii. 31, 32.

" O thou invisible spirit of wine, if thou hast no name to be known by, let us call thee devil.

" O that men should put an enemy in their mouths to steal away their brains." *Othello*, Act ii. Sc. 3.

"There shall no evil happen to the just; but the wicked shall be filled with mischief." *Prov.* xii. 21.

" What stronger breastplate than a heart untainted?
Thrice is he arm'd that has his quarrel just!
And he but naked, though locked up in steel,
Whose conscience with injustice is corrupted."

2 *Henry VI.*, Act iii. Sc. 2.

" What I speak,
My body shall make good upon the earth,
Or my divine soul answer it in heaven."

Richard II., i. 1.

" I say unto you, that every idle word that men shall speak, they shall give account thereof in the day of judgment."

Matthew xii. 36.

" Here we feel but the penalty of Adam."

As You Like It, Act ii. Sc. 1.

7

"The Lord God sent Adam forth from the garden of Eden to till the ground."   *Genesis* iii.

"Now, Lord, be thanked for my good amends."
                                    Taming of the Shrew.

"And he shall make amends for the harm he hath done."
                                    Leviticus v.

"Thus saith the Lord of Hosts, the God of Israel, Amend your ways."   *Jeremiah* vii.

"There is, sure, another flood toward, and these
    Couples are coming to the ark."
                                    As You Like It, Act v. Sc. 4.

"There went in two and two unto Noah into the ark, the male and female, as God had commanded Noah."
                                    Genesis vii.

"So Holy Writ in babes hath judgment shown,
    When judges have been babes."
                                    All's Well that Ends Well, Act ii. Sc.1.

"Some say, that ever 'gainst that season comes,
    Wherein our Saviour's birth is celebrated,
    The bird of dawning singeth all night long,
    So hallowed, and so gracious is the time."
                                    Hamlet, Act i. Sc. 1.

"Now when Jesus was born in Bethlehem of Judea, in the days of Herod the king, behold there came wise men from the east to Jerusalem, saying, Where is He that is born King of the Jews? for we have seen His star in the east, and are come to worship Him."   *Matthew* ii.

"If ever I were traitor,
    My name be blotted from the book of life,
    And I from heaven banish'd as from hence."
                                    Richard II., Act i. Sc. 3.

" He that overcometh, the same shall be clothed in white raiment, and I will not blot his name out of the book of life."
Revelation iii.

" With Cain, go wander through the shade of night,
And never show thy head by day nor night."
Richard II., Act v. Sc. 6.

" Behold, Thou hast driven me out this day from the face of the earth; and from Thy face shall I be hid; and I shall be a vagabond in the earth." *Genesis* iv.

" Heaven, lay not my transgression to my charge."
King John, Act i. Sc. 1.

" Lord, lay not this sin to their charge." *Acts* vii.

" Comfort's in heaven, we are on the earth."
Richard II., Act ii. Sc. 2.

" God is in heaven, and thou upon earth."
Ecclesiastes v.

"This sorrow's heavenly;
It strikes, where it doth love."
Othello, Act v. Sc. 2.

" Whom the Lord loveth, He correcteth." *Proverbs* iv.

" All that live, must die,
Passing through nature to eternity."
Hamlet, Act i. Sc. 2.

" As sin hath reigned unto death, even so might grace reign through righteousness unto eternal life." *Romans* v.

" All places that the eye of heaven visits,
Are to a wise man, ports and happy havens."
Richard II., Act i. Sc. 2.

" A land which the Lord God careth for; the eyes of the Lord

thy God are always upon it, from the beginning of the year even
unto the end of the year."   *Deut.* xi.

> " Then, heaven, set ope thy everlasting gates,
>   To entertain my vows of thanks and praise."
>   2 *Henry VI.*, Act iv. Sc. 9.

" Lift up your heads, O ye gates; and be ye lift up, ye everlasting doors, and the King of Glory shall come in."
                                                Psalm xxiv.

> " For in the book of Numbers it is writ,
>   When the man dies, let the inheritance
>   Descend unto the daughter."
>   *Henry V.*, Act i. Sc. 2.

" And thou shalt speak unto the children of Israel, saying, If
a man die, and have no son, then ye shall cause his inheritance
to pass unto his daughter."   *Numbers* xxvii.

> "Forbear to judge, for we are sinners all."
>   2 *Henry VI.*, Act iii. Sc. 3.

"Judge not, that ye be not judged; for with what judgment
ye judge, ye shall be judged."   *Matthew* vii. 1, 2.

> " O God! I fear thy justice will take hold
>   On me for this."   *Richard III.*, Act ii. Sc. 1.

> " Here, take you this,
>   And seal the bargain with a holy kiss."
>   *Two Gentlemen of Verona*, Act ii. Sc. 2.

" Salute one another with an holy kiss."
                                            Romans xvi. 16.

> " I myself will lead a private life,
>   And in devotion spend my latter days,
>   To sin's rebuke, and my Creator's praise."
>   3 *Henry VI.*, Act iv. Sc. 6.

" Afterward shall the children of Israel return, and seek the Lord their God, and shall fear the Lord, and His goodness, in the latter days." *Hosea* iii. 5.

" Blessed are the peacemakers on earth."
2 Henry VI., Act ii. Sc. 1.

" Blessed are the peacemakers; for they shall be called the children of God." *Matthew* v. 9.

" I never see thy face, but I think on hell-fire, and Dives that lived in purple, for there he is in his robes, burning, burning."
1 Henry IV., Act iii. Sc. 1.

" There was a certain rich man, which was clothed in purple and fine linen, and fared sumptuously every day ; and in hell he lifted up his eyes, being in torments, and cried, Father Abraham, have mercy on me." *Luke* xvi. 19, 23, 24.

> " I see thy glory, like a shooting star,
> Fall to the base earth from the firmament."
> *Richard II.,* Act ii. Sc. 4.

> " And the stars of heaven fell unto the earth."
> *Revelation* vi.

> " Methinks, the truth should live from age to age,
> As 't were retailed to all posterity,
> Even to the general all-ending day."
> *Richard III.,* Act iii. Sc. 1.

> " O God ! thy arm was here !
> And not to us, but to thy arm alone,
> Ascribe we all . . . . take it, God,
> For it is only Thine."
> *Henry V.,* Act iv. Sc. 8.

" O sing unto the Lord a new song, for He hath done marvellous things; His right hand and His holy arm hath gotten Him the victory." *Psalm* xcviii.

7 *

"The will of heaven
Be done in this, and all things."
Henry VIII., Act i. Sc. 1.

"Thy will be done as in heaven, so in earth." *Luke* xi.

"Wisdom cries out in the streets, and no man regards it."
1 *Henry IV.*, Act i. Sc. 2.

"Wisdom crieth without, she uttereth her voice in the streets."
Proverbs i.

"The fool doth think he is wise, but the wise man knows himself to be a fool." *As You Like It*, Act v. Sc. 1.

"The way of a fool is right in his own eyes; but he that hearkeneth unto counsel is wise." *Proverbs* xii.

"I, that am cruel, am yet merciful."
Othello, Act v. Sc. 2.

"The tender mercies of the wicked are cruel."
Proverbs xii.

"I pardon him, as God shall pardon me."
Richard II., Act v. Sc. 3.

"Forgive, and ye shall be forgiven." *Luke* vi.

"Good name in man and woman,
Is the immediate jewel of their souls."
Othello, Act iii. Sc. 3.

"A good name is rather to be chosen than great riches."
Proverbs xxii.

"No night is now with hymn or carol blest."
Midsummer-Night's Dream, Act ii. Sc. 2.

"Ye shall have a song as in the night." *Isaiah* xxx.

> " Saw you not, even now, a blessed troop
> Invite me to a banquet; whose bright faces
> Cast thousand beams upon me like the sun?
> They promis'd me eternal happiness."
>
> *Henry VIII.*, Act iv. Sc. 2.

" He saw in a vision, evidently about the ninth hour of the day, an angel of God coming in to him, and saying unto him, Cornelius, thy prayers and thine alms are come up for a memorial before God." *Acts* x. 3, 4.

Having brought the parallel passages between Shakespeare and the Bible to a close, the author deems it necessary to add that they by no means convey to the reader the full extent of Shakespeare's indebtedness to the Bible for the many very beautiful sentences, and moral lessons, that are to be found in his works. There are in his plays upwards of one thousand passages, not alluded to by us, wherein scriptural names of persons, places, rulers, and heavenly objects are introduced as illustrations of his subject, and which could not be quoted under the head of "parallel passages."

That our readers may more particularly understand the nature of these passages, we annex a few, which, while they show the wonderful and profound knowledge Shakespeare had of the Bible, will also account for our omission of them here.

There are several passages wherein the name of "Father Abraham," and "Good old Abraham" is used; also allusions to Cain and Abel, in the manner of accusations, as for instance:

" Be thou cursed, Cain, to slay thy brother Abel."
 1 *Henry VI.*, Act i. Sc. 2.

The name of Adam is frequently used in the same manner. " Heaven — angels — the planets," etc., are in many instances used in the same manner as they are in the Bible. In 2 Henry VI., iii. 3, we find this line :

" O thou eternal mover of the heavens, etc."

The reader will find the same idea in Ps. xxxiii. In Hamlet, Act v. Scene 1, the word angel is introduced in a line precisely in the same sense as in Heb. 1.

In " Love's Labor's Lost," Act v. Scene 1, an allusion is made to Judas Maccabees, and Holofernes, taken from 2 Maccabees v., and Judith 4.

The word " commander," in " Two Gentlemen of Verona," Act iv. Scene 1, finds a parallel in its use, Isaiah lx. The word " crown " is frequently used by Shakespeare in a scriptural sense.

The word " death " is frequently used by Shakespeare, but in no one instance, at least to our knowledge, is it introduced improperly ; words of a solemn and holy meaning are never sacrilegiously used. Speaking of death, he says (King John, Act iv. Scene 2) :

" We cannot hold mortality's strong hand. . . .
 . . . .
Have I commandment on the pulse of Life ? "

The reader will find that Shakespeare has taken this beautiful idea of death from Job xii. 9 :

"The hand of the Lord hath wrought this, in whose hand is the soul of every living thing, and the breath of all mankind."

The word " mercy," so frequently used by Shakespeare, is most singularly and strikingly scriptural in its connection with the subject upon which he treats ; as for instance :

> " The quality of mercy is not strain'd, etc."
> *Merchant of Venice,* Act iv. Sc. **1.**

is evidently taken from a passage in Psalm lvii. **3** :

> " God shall send forth his mercy, etc."

The several passages wherein the word is used by Shakespeare, as in "Merchant of Venice," Act iv. Scene **1**; "Timon of Athens," Act iii. Scene 5, etc., find their counterpart in Luke vi., Matthew v., Romans **xi.** We have given these few passages wherein the word mercy is introduced by Shakespeare in a scriptural sense, but are by no means specimens of the numerous instances in which they are similarly used. The word itself is mentioned by Shakespeare, throughout his plays, upwards of one hundred and sixty times, two-thirds of them are introduced in golden sentences drawn with a prophetic spirit from the Bible. We have said there are upwards of one thousand passages in Shakespeare, not alluded to by us in the parallel passages given, nor in the biblical texts adopted by him, all of which, although not absolute quotations, are nevertheless borrowed from the sacred volume. The reader will perceive, from the few extracts we have given, how closely Shakespeare followed the Bible in composing his wonderful plays. The prophets of old were inspired by heaven to write the "Book of Books." Shakespeare was inspired by that Book to compose its counterpart. The one governs the world universally, the other the world in miniature. It has been said of Shakespeare, speaking of his genius, that it is delightful to behold him, while depicting the sublunary scenes of human life in all its various shades, exhorting us, at the same time, to look up with adoration to the Omnipotent Creator of the universe.

BIBLICAL TEXTS ADOPTED BY SHAKE-
SPEARE.

THE following passages from Shakespeare are given for the purpose of showing how closely he adhered to the spirit of the Bible, by clothing the sublimity of thoughts and ideas contained in that Holy Book, in language and words of his own. Thus it will be seen that many beautiful passages attributed to him can be traced directly to the Scriptures. It is, therefore, very evident that Shakespeare at a very early age must have been strongly imbued with the pure morality of the Bible, and his mind tinctured with Divine truth.

He has been termed the text for the moralist and the philosopher; but is he not the exponent of a greater text-book, and not the sole creator of the beauties which make up the "mimic world" of which he is the acknowledged ruler? Even here the might of a higher power is evident. "Shakespeare and the Bible," are so frequently coupled together that the

83

enthusiasts of the former seem ready to worship at his shrine. Think, O man, with whom you compare Shakespeare. What is he, or a million like him, to the " Great I Am " of the universe ? All earthly things are

> . . . . " As a drop of water in the sea,
> All this magnificence in thee is lost:
> What are ten thousand worlds compared to THEE ?
>> Heaven's unnumbered host,
> Though multiplied by myriads, and arrayed
> In all the glory of sublimest thought,
> Is but an atom in the balance weighed
> Against thy greatness, is a cipher brought
> Against infinity." *Derzhavin.*

> " Heaven doth with us as we with torches do —
>> Not light them for themselves ; for if our virtues
>> Did not go forth of us, etc."
>> *Measure for Measure,* Act i. Sc. 1.

" Neither do men light a candle, and put it under a bushel, but on a candlestick; and it giveth light unto all that are in the house.

" Let your light so shine before men, that they may see your good works." *Matthew* v. 15, 16.

> " What stronger breastplate than a heart untainted."
>> 2 *King Henry VI.,* Act iii. Sc. 2.

" Stand therefore, having your loins girt about with truth, and having on the breastplate of righteousness."
>> *Ephesians* vi. 14.

> . . . . " How in one house,
> Should many people, under two commands,
> Hold amity ? " *King Lear,* Act ii. Sc. 4.

"No man can serve two masters." *Matthew* vi. 24.

> "Wisdom and goodness to the vile seem vile,
> Filths savor but themselves."
>
> *King Lear*, Act iv. Sc. 2.

"Unto the pure all things are pure; but unto them that are defiled and unbelieving *is* nothing pure." *Titus* i. 15.

> "It is the purpose that makes strong the vow;
> But vows to every purpose must not hold."
>
> *Troilus and Cressida*, Act v. Sc. 3.

"Better is it that thou should'st not vow, than that thou should'st vow, and not pay." *Eccl.* v. 5.

"Put not your trust in princes, nor in the son of man, in whom there is no help." *Psalm* cxlvi. 3.

> "O, how wretched
> Is that poor man that hangs on princes' favors.
>
> *King Henry VIII.*, Act iii. Sc. 2.

"He answered and said unto them, When it is evening, ye say, it will be fair weather; for the sky is red."

Matthew xvi. 2.

> "The weary sun hath made a golden set,
> And by the bright track of his fiery car,
> Gives token of a goodly day to-morrow."
>
> *Richard III.*, Act v. Sc. 3.

"They that mean virtuously, and yet do so,
The devil their virtue tempts, and they tempt heaven."

Othello, Act iv. Sc. 1.

"Jesus said unto him, It is written again, Thou shalt not tempt the Lord thy God." *Matthew* iv. 7.

> "God's benison go with you; and with those
> That would make good of bad, and friends of foes."
>
> *Macbeth*, Act ii. Sc. 4.

8

" Blessed are the peacemakers ; for they shall be called the children of God."   *Matthew* v. 9.

> " Blood, like sacrificing Abel's, cries,
> Even from the tongueless caverns of the earth."
> *King Richard II.*, Act i. Sc. 1.

" And he said, What hast thou done ? the voice of thy brother's blood crieth unto me from the ground."
                                                        Genesis iv. 10.

> " Withhold thine indignation, mighty Heaven,
> And tempt us not to bear above our power."
> *King John*, Act v. Sc. 6.

" There hath no temptation taken you but such as is common to man ; but God *is* faithful, who will not suffer you to be tempted above that ye are able, but will with the temptation also make a way to escape, that ye may be able to bear it."
                                                        1 *Cor.* x. 13.

> " Heaven, the widow's champion and defence."
> *Richard II.*, Act i. Sc. 1.

" Ye shall not afflict any widow, or fatherless child. If thou afflict them in any wise, and they cry at all unto me, I will surely hear their cry."   *Exodus* xxii. 22, 23.

In the following passage, it shows that Shakespeare had a most correct idea of the nature of Divine sovereignty :

> " The words of Heaven ; on whom it will, it will ;
> On whom it will not, so ; yet still 't is just."   aaɛa
> *Measure for Measure*, Act i. Sc. 3.

" For he saith to Moses, I will have mercy on whom I will have mercy, and I will have compassion on whom I will have compassion."   *Romans* ix. 15.

> . . . "For honor —
> 'T is derivative from me to mine,
> And only that I stand for."
> *Winter's Tale*, Act iii. Sc. 2.

"The glory of a man is from the honor of his father."
Ecclesiasticus iii. 2.

"All offences come from the heart."
King Henry V., Act iv. Sc. 8.

"But those things which proceed out of the mouth come forth from the heart; and they defile the man. For out of the heart proceed evil thoughts, murders, adulteries, fornications, thefts, false witness, blasphemies." *Matthew* xv. 18, 19.

"But godliness with contentment is great gain."
1 *Timothy* vi. 6.

"Poor and content, is rich, and rich enough."
Othello, Act iii. Sc. 3.

"A foolish son is a grief to his father, and a bitterness to his mother." *Prov.* xvii. 25.

"How sharper than a serpent's tooth it is to have a thankless child." *King Lear*, Act i. Sc. 4.

"Nature teaches beasts to know their friends."
Coriolanus ii. 1.

"The ox knoweth his owner, and the ass his master's crib."
Isaiah i. 3.

> "A good and virtuous nature may recoil
> In an imperial charge." *Macbeth*, Act iv. Sc. 3.

Of the truth of this, Hazael, King of Syria, affords a striking instance. See 2 Kings viii. 12, 13.

"As stars with trains of fire and dews of blood."
Hamlet, Act i. Sc. 1.

" The stars in their course fought against Sisera."

Judges v. 20.

" That undiscovered country from whose bourne
No traveller returns." *Hamlet*, Act iii. Sc. 1.

" Man goeth to his long home." *Ecclesiastes* xii. 6.

" I have begun to plant thee, and will labor
To make thee full of growing."

Macbeth, Act i. Sc. 4.

" I have planted, Apollos watered; but God gave the increase." 1 *Cor.* iii. 6.

The celebrated curse in Lear, of which so much is said, both for and against (Act i. Scene 4), may with propriety be traced to Psalm cix. 1–15.

Shakespeare, in several of his plays, has shown that if ambitious persons had had patience, they would not have been led to crime, and catastrophes had never befallen them. If in this light we consider " Othello," " Lear," " Macbeth," " Cymbeline," " Henry VII.," " The Winter's Tale," " Julius Cæsar," " Timon of Athens," etc., we shall see that a want of patience has been the cause of almost all the wickedness and misfortune which happened to them. See how beautifully patience is illustrated in the book of Job, for the Lord gave him twice as much as he had before :

" So the Lord blessed the latter end of Job more than his beginning, etc."

His afflictions were terminated, his reputation

and honor were restored. All his relations and neigh-
bors, who had before treated him with disdain, on
account of his poverty, now came around him.
They condoled with and comforted him. Thus the
patience of Job brought about a new era in his life,
for he lived a hundred and forty years, and saw his
sons, and his sons' sons even four generations:

"So Job died, being old and full of years."   xlii. 17.

Shakespeare says, "Have patience and endure."
Thomson thus beautifully defines it:

"From savage Nature,
'T is patience that has built up human life,
The nurse of arts; and Rome exalts her head,
An everlasting monument of patience."

"And God said, Let us make man in our image, after our
likeness, and let them have dominion over the fish of the sea,
and over the fowl of the air, and over the cattle, and over all
the earth, and over every creeping thing that creepeth upon the
earth."   *Genesis* i. 26.

Shakespeare, in his "Comedy of Errors," Act ii.,
paraphrases this passage, showing man's preëminence
over all other created things, "the beasts, the fishes,
and the winged fowls," etc.

"Created
Of every creature's best."
                              Tempest, Act iii. Sc. 1.

"Shall we desire to raze the sanctuary
And pitch our evils there?"
                         Measure for Measure, Act ii.

8*

" And they brake down the image of Baal and brake down
the house of Baal, and made it a draught house unto this day."

2 Kings x. 27.

> " Give me that man
> That is not passion's slave, and I will wear him
> In my heart's core, ay, in my heart of heart,
> As I do thee."   *Hamlet*, Act iii. Sc. 2.

" A man after his own heart."   1 *Samuel* xiii. 14.

> " My way of life
> Is fallen into the sere, the yellow leaf."
>
> *Macbeth*, Act iv. Sc 3.

" We all do fade as a leaf."   *Isaiah* lxiv. 6.

Polonius' advice to his son (on his taking leave of
his eccentric parent to pursue his travels abroad), finds
a parallel in Ecclesiasticus xxix. 1–28.

Cleopatra's dream, in " Antony and Cleopatra," is
evidently taken from Revelation.   She says :

> " His face was as the heavens, and therein stuck
> A sun, and moon; which kept their course, and lighted
> The little O, the earth," etc.

If Shakespeare intended the dream to apply to Antony, comparing him to a spirit of light, whose face
" was as the heavens," it was an oversight, and his judgment must have been carried away with the subject.
Act v. Scene 2.

The reverence paid to Christmas time is thus beautifully described by Shakespeare, in which the reader
will find an allusion to our Saviour's birth:

> " It faded on the crowing of the cock,
> Some say, that ever 'gainst that season comes
> Wherein our Saviour's birth is celebrated,
> This bird of dawning singeth all night long:
> And then, they say, no spirit can walk abroad."
>
> *Hamlet*, Act i.

Shakespeare's reading and study of the Bible did not limit itself to the Old and New Testament alone, but he studied with equal care and attention the Apocrypha. The general idea of the epilogue to the comedy of " As You Like It," is evidently taken from the last two verses of the second book of Maccabees. The celebrated phrase, " good wine needs no bush," may be traced to that book.

Hamlet's soliloquy on the skull of Yorick, where he says, " Now, get you to my lady's chamber," etc., finds a parallel in the concluding verses of the third chapter of the book of Isaiah.

The reader will find a striking similarity between a passage in Job and Macbeth. It is where both receive the various messengers announcing evil tidings. A reference to the fifth act of Macbeth, Scenes 3 and 5, will show that Shakespeare had Job in his " mind's eye" when he wrote these scenes. There is also in Richard something similar, but not so striking.

There is another passage in Macbeth which has been frequently quoted for its beauty and depth of pathos and feeling :

> " Out, out, brief candle!
> Life 's but a walking shadow; a poor player,
> That struts and frets his hour upon the stage,
> And then is heard no more: it is a tale
> Told by an idiot, full of sound and fury,
> Signifying nothing."   Act v. Sc. 5.

" For all our days are passed away in thy wrath: we spend our years as *a tale that is told.*"   *Ps.* xc. 9.

> " This is the state of man: to-day he puts forth
> The tender leaves of hopes, to-morrow blossoms,
> . . . . The third day comes a frost, a killing frost;
> And,— when he thinks, good easy man, full surely
> His greatness is a ripening,— nips his root,
> And then he falls, as I do."
>   *Henry VIII.*, Act iii. Sc. 2.

" In the morning it flourisheth, and groweth up; in the evening it is cut down, and withereth."   *Ps.* xc. 6.

> " I will not yield,
> To kiss the ground before young Malcolm's feet, etc."
>   *Macbeth*, Act v. Sc. 7.

" They that dwell in the wilderness shall bow before him, and his enemies shall lick the dust."

> " In time to come."   *Deut.* v. 20.

> " In my time to come."
> *Merry Wives of Windsor*, Act iii. Sc. 4.

" Thou died before thy time."   *Eccl.* vii. 17.

" She should have died hereafter."
                    Macbeth, Act v. Sc. 5.

Shakespeare's use of the word "time" in connection with a sentence, is truly scriptural. "In time to come'' is repeatedly found in the Bible, and Shakespeare, in many passages, adheres closely to the peculiar, and we may say, inspired manner of its scriptural use. Let us give a few of the Bible sentences in which it is found : '' Asketh thee in time to come,'' Exodus xiii. 14; this is repeated word for word in Deut. vi. 20. '' In time to come,'' Josh. iv. 21. '' In time to come,'' Prov. xxxi. 25. '' The time to come,'' Isaiah xxx. 8. '' Time to come,'' 1 Tim. vi. 19. All words of this kind which have a positive meaning, emphatic, and intended to illustrate some striking lesson, are frequently used by Shakespeare in exactly the manner and style of the Bible. We have another word equally striking as that of time — '' everlasting.'' Shakespeare uses it, '' Everlasting fire,'' in '' Titus Andronicus.'' '' Everlasting bonfire light,'' 1 *Henry IV.*, Act iii. Scene 3. '' Everlasting bonfire,'' *Macbeth*, Act ii. Scene 3.

We find a similar passage in Matthew xxv. 41, '' *Everlasting fire.*'' In Isaiah xxxiii. 14, '' *Everlasting burnings.*''

All these applications are to a future state of punishment, while others again are to '' everlasting life,'' etc.

> '' Thy voice his dreadful thunder.''
> *Love's Labor's Lost*, Act iv. Sc. 2.

'' The voice of thy thunder.'' *Psalm* lxxvii. 13.

'' The voice of a great thunder.'' *Rev.* xiv. 2.

> '' With all his might.''
> *Merry Wives of Windsor*, Act ii. Sc. 1.

" With all his might."   *Deut.* vi. 5.

" I 'm very sure,
If they should speak, would almost damn those ears,
Which hearing them would call their brother's fools."
Merchant of Venice.

Alluding to the Scripture text, "He that calleth his brother a fool," etc.

How truly scriptural is the following:

" Ay, but to die, and go we know not where;
To lie in cold obstruction, and to rot."
Measure for Measure, Act iii. Sc. 1.

" The sure and firm earth
Hear not my steps, which way they walk, for fear
The very stones prate of my whereabouts."
Macbeth, Act ii. Sc. 1.

"And Joshua said unto all the people, Behold, this stone shall be a witness unto us, for it hath heard all the words of the Lord, which he spake unto us."   *Joshua* xxiv. 27.

" The stone shall cry out of the wall."   *Habakkuk* ii. 11.

"Wo unto him, that saith to the wood, Awake; to the dumb stone, Arise, it shall teach."   ver. 19.

There are many passages in Shakespeare which have a direct bearing upon scriptural subjects, such as, "It was Eve's legacy," etc. (*Two Gentlemen of Verona*, Act iii. Scene 1.)

In another portion of our work, we have given similar expressions used rather loosely by Falstaff.

In Macbeth, we find this passage:

> " Macbeth
> Is ripe for shaking, and the powers above
> Put on their instruments."

Instruments here, is meant to gird on their swords. So used in Psalm vii. 12, 13 :

" If a man will not turn, he will whet his sword; he hath bent his bow, and made it ready. He hath prepared for him the instruments of death; he ordaineth his arrows against the persecutors."

SHAKESPEARE AND THE CLASSICS.

IT is not our purpose to point out parallel passages between Shakespeare and other writers prior to the production of his plays; indeed, such a task would be superfluous, as the instances are so few, and the similarities so obscure. The following, however, we give, as they show that his reading was far more extensive than certain commentators gave him credit. Some speeches in Shakespeare's "Coriolanus" are not more than metrical arrangements of the very words in Sir Thomas North's translation of "Plutarch's Lives," first published in 1579:

"I am Caius Martius, who hath done to thyself particularly, and to all the Volsces generally, great hurt and mischiefe, which I cannot denie for my surname of Coriolanus that I beare. For I never had other benefit nor recompense of the true and painefull services I have done, and the extreme dangers I have bene in, but this onely surname; a good memorie and witnesse of the malice and displeasure thou shouldest bear me. Indeed, the name only remaineth with me; for the rest, the envie and crueltie of the people of Rome have taken from me, by the sufferance of the dastardly nobilitie and magistrates, who have forsaken me, and let me be banished by the people. That extremitie hath now driven me to come as a poor suitor, to take thy chimnie harth, not of any hope to save my life thereby. For if I had feared death, I would not have come hither to have put myself in hazard."—*North's Plutarch*, folio, p. 232.

> " My name is Caius Marcius, who hath done
> To thee particularly, and to all the Volsces,
> Great hurt and mischief, thereto witness may
> My surname Coriolanus: The painful service,
> The extreme dangers, and the drops of blood
> Shed for my thankless country, are requited
> But with that surname: a good memory,
> And witness of the malice and displeasure
> Which thou should'st bear me: only that name remains;
> The cruelty and envy of the people,
> Permitted by our dastard nobles, who
> Have all forsook me, hath devour'd the rest;
> And suffered me by the voice of slaves to be
> Whoop'd out of Rome. Now, this extremity
> Hath brought me to thy hearth; not out of hope;
> Mistake me not, to save my life; for if
> I had feared death, of all men i' the world,
> I would have 'voided thee." *Coriolanus*, Act iv. Sc. 5.

" Sea of troubles," is from the Greek Ηιλαγος Καχων. Many of the commentators of Shakespeare contend that it should read " *siege* " of troubles. We think the Greek authority should settle the question.

> " *Hoc sustinete, majus ne veniat malum.*"

" Bear with, submit to, put up with this misfortune, lest a greater should befall you." *Latin Phædrus.*

9   G

Shakespeare says :

" Better to bear the ills we have, than fly to others that we know not of."

Plautus uses the following :

" I do sincerely believe my wife to be most virtuous."

This reminds us strongly of a similar passage in Othello.

" Natio comoeda est."   *Latin Juvenal.*

" The whole nation appears like a set of stage-players — there every one is an actor."   "Greece is a theatre where all are players."

> " All the world 's a stage,
> And all the men and women merely players."
>
> *Shakespeare.*

> " Is the warlike sound of drum and trump turned
> To the soft notes of lyre and lute?   The neighing
> Of barbed steeds, whose loudness filled the air with
> Terror, and whose breaths dimmed the sun with
> Smoke, converted to delicate tunes and
> Amorous glances?"
>
> *Lyly's Alexander and Campaspe,* 1584.

> " Grim-visag'd war hath smoothed his wrinkled front,
> And now, instead of mounting barbed steeds
> To fright the souls of fearful adversaries,
> He capers nimbly in a lady's chamber,
> To the lascivious pleasing of a lute."
>
> *Richard III.,* 1591.

> " Oh, sable night, sit on the eye of heaven,
> That it discern not this black deed of darkness."
>
> *Warning for Fair Women,* 1599.

Readers familiar with Shakespeare will remember this passage in Macbeth, Act iii. Scene 2 :

> " Come seeling night,
> Scarf up the tender eye of pitiful day," etc.

" Oft does the mind wish for, desiderate, what it has missed, and loses itself in the retrospective contemplation." " Most men have occasion to look back with regret on their lost opportunities."   *From the Latin. Pretonius Arbiter.*

> " There is a tide in the affairs of men,
> Which, taken at the flood, leads on to fortune;
> Omitted, all the voyage of their life
> Is bound in shadows and in miseries."
> *Shakespeare.*

" Once lost, then prized." " The worth of a thing is best known by the want."   *French Proverb.*

> " That which we have we prize not to the worth
> While we enjoy it, but being lacked and lost,
> Why then we rack the value; then we find
> The value that possession would not give us."
> *Shakespeare.*

" So long as you are in good circumstances, you will number, reckon up, many friends; but, if the times change with you, if you get on your beam ends, then will you find yourself alone in the world."   *From the Latin. Ovid.*

> " Where you are liberal of your loves and counsels,
> Be sure you do not lose; for those you make friends,
> And give your hearts to, when they once perceive
> The least rub in your fortunes, fall away
> Like water from ye, never found again,
> But where they mean to sink ye."   *Shakespeare.*

> " *Est quædam fiere voluptas*
> *Expletur lacrimis, egeriturque dolor.*"
> " There is a certain pleasure in weeping," etc.   *Ovid.*

Shakespeare tells us, " There is a luxury in grief." " Double, double, toil and trouble," as used by Thomas Middleton and Shakespeare, can be traced to Sophocles. *Ajax*, I. 824.

> " My voice stuck in my throat."   *Virgil.*

> " And amen
> Stuck in my throat."   *Macbeth.*

" She nourishes the poison in the veins, and is consumed by the hidden fire."   *Virgil.*

> " But let concealment, like a worm i' th' bud,
> Feed on her damask cheek."   *Twelfth Night.*

In Marlowe's " Edward II." (1593), we find the following :

> " Gallop a pace bright Phœbus through the sky,
> And dusky night in rusty iron car,
> Between you both shorten the time I pray,
> That I may see that most desired day."

Compare this with a passage in " Romeo and Juliet " (1597) :

> " Gallop a pace, you fiery-footed steeds,
> Towards Phœbus' mansion ; such a wagoner
> As Phæton would whip you to the west,
> And bring in cloudy night immediately."

Malone imagined that the " Romeo and Juliet " of

Shakespeare was designed in the year 1591, but not finished until 1596. Chalmer refers to it 1592, and Dr. Drake 1593. There are four editions of it in quarto, namely, those of 1597, 1599, 1609, and one without date.

In Act iv. Sc. 1 of "Measure for Measure," Shakespeare has inserted the first stanzas of a very beautiful sonnet, which Malone has published entire in "The Passionate Pilgrim." The sonnet is well known; we transcribe it, for the purpose of comparing it with some lyric lines of Gallus, a poet of the Augustan age:

> " Take, oh! take those lips away,
> That so sweetly were foresworn;
>   And those eyes, the break of day,
> Lights that do mislead the morn;
>   But my kisses bring again,
>   Seals of love, but sealed in vain.
> Hide, oh! hide those hills of snow
>   Which thy frozen bosom bears;
> On whose tops the pinks that grow
>   Are of those that April wears;
> But first set my poor heart free,
> Bound in those icy chains by thee."

In an edition of Catullus, Tiburtius, Propertius, and the fragment of Gallus, published at Venice, 1558, are the following lines:

> " Lida bella puella candita,
>   Quæ bene fnperas lac, et lilium,
>   Albamq; fimul rosam rubidam,
>   Aut expolitum ebur Indicum.

9 *

Pande puella, pande capillulos
  Flavos, lucentes ut aurum nitidum
  Pande puella collum candidum,
  Productum bene candidis humoris.

Pande puella stellatos oculos,
  Flexaq; super mgra cilia,
Pande puella genas roseas,
  Perfusas rubro purpuræ Tyriæ."

The terrible curse of "Lear," Act i. Sc. 4, commencing with, "Hear, Nature, hear, dear goddess,
hear," although standing alone in the vast library of
English literature, has a very remarkable and noble
parallel in that of Œdipus upon his sons, in the
"Œdipus Coloneus" of Sophocles. A writer says:
"There is not the remotest probability that the Greek
drama was in any way known to Shakespeare, as whatever might have been the precise extent of his literary
acquirements, Greek tragedy was certainly not within
their limits, and Sophocles had not then been translated."

The similarity consists, not so much in imitation,
even if Shakespeare had read the tragedy, but the
resemblance is that of deep passion, and that of imagery. It is, perhaps, the most remarkable coinci-
dence of genius in distant ages that is to be found in
the record of letters.

"Whilst there is life there is hope." This is from
the Latin of Cicero. The full expression, however, is:
"*Aegroto dum vita est, spes est,*" "Whilst, or so
long as, the sick man is alive, he may hope to re-
cover."

> " The miserable have no other medicine,
> But only hope."   *Shakespeare.*

" The injury done to character is greater than can possibly be estimated."   *Livy.*

> " Good name in man or woman, dear my lord,
> Is the immediate jewel of their soul.
> Who steals my purse steals trash;
> 'T is something, nothing; 'T was mine, 't is his,
> And has been slave to thousands;
> But he who filches from me my good name,
> Robs me of that which not enriches him,
> And makes me poor indeed."   *Shakespeare.*

" Much is wanting to those that seek or covet much."
                                              Horace.

> " Poor and content, is rich and rich enough;
> But riches, fineless, is as poor as winter,
> To him that ever fears he shall be poor."
                                          Shakespeare.

" All things are capturable, seizable, may be done, managed, accomplished by application and toil, labor, exertion, trouble."
                                              Menander.

" Nothing is so difficult but by industry it may be accomplished."   *Terrence.*

" Every thing may be discovered, if we do not shun the necessary labor, which however is generally the attendant of those who are engaged in difficult researches and investigations."   *Philomon, an Athenian Poet.*

If Shakespeare read but one of the above authors quoted, he found material enough to compose the following:

" Do not for one repulse, forego the purpose
That you resolved to effect."

Tempest, Act iii. Sc. 3.

" Make not impossible that which seems unlike."

Measure for Measure, Act v. Sc. 1.

" I gave him fifteen wounds,
Which now be fifteen mouths that do accuse me;
In every mouth there is a bloody tongue
Which will speak although he holds his peace."

A Warning for Fair Women (1599).

Compare this with " Antony and Cleopatra : "

" Show you sweet Cæsar's wounds, poor, poor dumb
mouths, etc."   Act iii. Sc. 2.

" And put a tongue
In every wound of Cæsar's, etc." (1607).

In the same play alluded to above, there is this
passage :

" Now is the hour come
To put your love unto the touch; to try
If it be current, or base counterfeit."

Compare it with the following in Richard III. :

" Now do I play the touch
To try if thou be current gold indeed." *

---

* Collier, speaking of " A Warning for Fair Women," which
was printed 1599, says: " Its resemblance to Shakespeare's
plays is not merely verbal; the speeches of Anne Sandus, the
repentant wife, are Shakespearian in a much better sense. But
for the extreme rarity of this tragedy, it might ere now have
been attributed to Shakespeare."

COINCIDENCES OR EXPRESSIONS TO BE FOUND IN BACON AND SHAKESPEARE.

POETRY is nothing else but feigned history."

Bacon.

"'T is poetical.   It is the more likely to be feigned."
"The truest poetry is the most feigning."

Shakespeare.

"He that builds a fair house upon an ill seat committeth himself to prison; nor do I reckon that an ill seat only where the air is unwholesome, but likewise where it is unequal."   *Bacon.*

"This castle hath a pleasant seat — the air,
Nimbly and sweet, recommends itself
Unto our gentle senses."   *Shakespeare.*

"Behaviour seemeth to me a garment of the mind, and to have the condition of a garment, for it ought to be made in fashion, and ought not to be curious."   *Bacon,* 1605.

"Costly thy habit as thy purse can buy,
But not express'd in fancy; rich not gaudy."

Shakespeare, 1603.

105

" Is not the opinion of Aristotle worthy to be regarded, where he saith, that young men are not fit auditors of moral philosophy ? " *Bacon*, 1605.

> " Unlike young men, whom Aristotle thought
> Unfit to hear moral philosophy."
>
> *Shakespeare*, 1609.

" In the third place, I set down reputation, because of the peremptory tides and currents it hath, which, if they be not taken in due time, are seldom recovered; it being extremely hard to play an after game of reputation." *Bacon*, 1605.

> " There is a tide in the affairs of men,
> Which, taken at the flood, leads on to fortune;
> Omitted, all the voyage of their life
> Is bound in shadows and in miseries."
>
> *Shakespeare*, 1603.

Bacon relates that a fellow, named Hog, importuned Sir Nicholas to save his life on account of the kindred between Hog and Bacon.

" Aye, but," replied the judge, " you and I cannot be kindred except you be hanged; for Hog is not Bacon until it will be hanged."

In " Merry Wives of Windsor," Shakespeare alludes to the same joke :

> *Evans.*— " Hung, hang, hog."
> *D. Quickly.*—" Hang-hog is the Latin for Bacon."

" For these be wise men that have secret hearts, but transparent countenances." *Bacon.*

> " And the whiteness in thy cheek
> Is apter than thy tongue to tell thy errand."
>
> *Shakespeare.*

" Yet evermore it must be remembered, that the least part of knowledge passed to man by this so large a charter from God, must be subject to that use for which God hath granted it, which is the benefit and relief of the state and·society of man."

Bacon, 1620.

> . . . . " Nature never lends
> The smallest scruple of her excellence;
> But, like a thrifty goddess, she determines
> Herself the glory of a creditor,
> Both use and knowledge." *Shakespeare,* 1604.

" As his victory gave him the knee, so his purposed marriage with the Lady Elizabeth gave him the heart, so that both knee and heart did truly bow before him." *Bacon,* 1622.

> "Show heaven the humbled heart, and not the knee."
> *Richard II.,* 1597.

> " And crook the pregnant hinges of the knee."
> *Hamlet,* 1602.

"Some books are to be tasted, others to be swallowed, and digested." *Bacon,* 1605.

> " How shall we stretch our eyes,
> When capital crimes, chewed, swallowed, and digested,
> Appear before us ? " *Shakespeare,* 1598.

" And therefore, in conclusion, he wished him not to shut the gate of your Majesty's mercy against himself, by being obdurate any longer." *Bacon.*

> " The gates of mercy shall shut up."
> *Shakespeare.*

" It is better they should be graced with elegancy, than daubed with cost." *Bacon.*

> "Poor Tom's a cold : I cannot daub it further."
> *Shakespeare.*

" All was inned at last into the king's barn." *Bacon.*

> " He that ears my land spares my team,
> And gives me leave to inn my crop."
>
> *Shakespeare.*

" It is more pleasing to have a lively work upon a sad and solemn ground, than to have a dark and melancholy work upon a lightsome ground." *Bacon.*

> " Bright metals on a sullen ground
> Will show more goodly, and attract more eyes,
> Than that which hath no foil to set off."
>
> *Shakespeare.*

> " The flesh shrinketh, but the bones resisteth,
> Whereby the cold becometh more eager."
>
> *Bacon,* 1612.

Hamlet.— " The air bites shrewdly — it is very cold.
Horatio.— It is a nipping and an eager air."

> *Shakespeare,* 1597.

" For the sound will greater or lesser, as the barrel is more empty or more full." *Bacon,* 1612.

> " Nor are these empty-hearted, whose low sound
> Reverts no hollowness." *Shakespeare,* 1606.

In Act ii. Sc. 1 of Henry VI., we find this passage:

Glou.— " My lord, 't is but a base, ignoble mind,
That mounts no higher than a bird can soar."

There is a Latin sentence somewhat similar, the translation of which is, " Hope soars beyond an eagle's flight."

As Shakespeare and Bacon were the two great writers

of the period in which they lived, it is not to be wondered at that a similarity of thought and expression should be found in their writings. It will be observed, however, that it is only in the philosophical these parallelisms are discernible, for in that of the dramatic Shakespeare stands alone. Bacon bathed in the " pool of philosophy," Shakespeare in that of the drama.

10

PRAYERS ON THE STAGE.

THE Rev. James Plumptre, B. D., Fellow of Clare Hall, England, speaking of "Prayers on the Stage," in the Great St. Mary's Church, Cambridge, on Sunday, September 25, 1808, says:

"Another instance of the profaneness of the stage is in prayers addressed to false objects, or in prayers addressed to the true God in an improper manner. Writers and performers, with a view, perhaps, to avoid the seeming impiety of addressing the Deity in that, which was but a representation, a fiction, have run into the other impiety of offering a feigned prayer to a feigned object, and thus making light of that awful and necessary duty. Many, indeed, have doubted and denied the propriety of addressing Deity in representations, because they are not realities. But if a character be introduced, as an example for our imitation, in such circumstances as, were he in real life, trust in God and prayer to him would be a duty, provided it be done with reverence, it does not appear to be a mockery, and in vain, but a highly useful lesson. Are we not too little accustomed, too much ashamed, to let ourselves be seen, or known to be on our knees before God in real life? We are commanded, indeed, not to pray in public, for the sake of being seen by men (Matt. vi. 5), for the motive ought to be to please God : but we are commanded to 'let our light so shine before men, that they may see our good works, and GLORIFY OUR FATHER WHO IS IN HEAVEN.'" (Matt. v. 16.)

Mrs. More, speaking upon the subject, says : " It is, perhaps, one of the most invincible objections to many tragedies, otherwise not very exceptionable, that the awful and tremendous name of the infinitely glorious God is shamefully and almost incessantly introduced in various scenes, both in the way of asseveration and of invocation."

" The next charge which equally rests against almost all theatrical exhibitions, is the horrid profanation of THE SACRED NAME OF GOD. Whether our minds ought to be more disgusted at the light and frothy style in which the comedian sports with that SACRED NAME, or whether the like profaneness adopted in the solemn grimace of tragedy may not be still more offensive than the former, might be difficult to determine. For can anything be more shocking, than when the tragic actor at times can bend his knee in his mock devotions, as in the presence of the eternal God, in language apparently the most solemn, though on a subject perhaps the most insulting to the purity and holiness of the divine existence."—*R. Hill's Warning*, p. 16.

As an instance, we might quote a passage from "Hamlet," Act iii. Scene 3. Although we have seen it represented on the stage, it has of late years been discarded, and very justly, as it pictures a part of Hamlet's character contrary to the spirit of Christianity.

The scene is where the king is represented as stung with remorse on account of the discovery being made of his having murdered his brother, and his reflections thereon. Some of them are very good, and we refer the reader to the passage rather than quote them here. The king enters, and kneels, and continues for some time in that posture, praying, or rather endeavoring to pray silently; till, finding his soul too much distracted with a sense of his sin, he gives it up. During the scene Hamlet enters; and seeing him unguarded, would put him to death, but that he thinks killing him, whilst at his prayers, would be the means of sending him to heaven, and so his father would not be revenged.

Another instance of a character represented on the stage as praying, without the words being given, is in "Lady Jane Gray," in Act v. Scene 2. She is discovered kneeling, as at her devotion; a light and a book placed on a table before her. Lord Guilford Dudley and two female attendants enter; one of them says to him:

> "Softly, my lord!
> For yet behold she kneels. Before the night
> Had reach'd her middle space, she left her bed,
> And with a pleasing, sober cheerfulness,

> As for her funeral, array'd herself
> In those sad, solemn weeds.   Since then her knee
> Has known that posture only, and her eye,
> Or fix'd upon the sacred page before her,
> Or lifted with her rising hopes to heav'n."

Macduff, after hearing of the murder of his wife and children by Macbeth, says:

> "Gentle heaven,
> Cut short all intermission; front to front,
> Bring thou this fiend of Scotland and myself;
> Within my sword's length set him; if he 'scape,
> Heaven forgive him too!"

This is perfectly justifiable; it is uttered under circumstances of grievous affliction, aggravation, and wrong. A learned writer of the stage speaking of this passage, says: "It is an unchristian wish, that Heaven may not forgive him; which, notwithstanding the injuries Macduff had sustained, is certainly an unchristian wish." Viewed perhaps calmly, and in the abstract, a serious writer might come to this conclusion, but for ourself we most seriously advocate its admission and toleration on the stage. An excellent writer, and able divine, speaking of this oath, remarks: "Even this is scarcely justified," and goes on to say, "I saw this play (Macbeth) acted at Covent Garden, in October, 1807, after some years' absence from all the theatres, during which time my ideas respecting plays had undergone very great changes. When the performer went down upon one

10 *   H

knee, and spoke this [the prayer], I felt very much shocked.''

Bishop of Lundaff's speech spoken, or was intended to have been spoken, in the House of Lords, November 22, 1803 [printed this year], contains the following :

" There is not an Admiral, an officer, a sailor, in the British navy, who does not burn with impatience to have an opportunity of attacking the enemy, France, who is not ready to exclaim with Macbeth,

> " Within my sword's length set him ; if he 'scape,
> May Heaven forgive him too.''

In the tragedy of the Regent, where Manuel, the supposed murderer of Dianord's husband, offers her the choice of submitting to his will, or having her child murdered, she says :

> "——Yet a moment pause !   (*Kneels.*)
> My Father and my God, O, thou of mercy,
> Look down, look down, upon the wretched'st woman
> That ever raised the imploring eyes of anguish,
> And guide her in her choice — choice !   Lose my boy ?
> Him, Maker whom thou gav'st me with sharp throes !
> No : let thy pity wash the stain away,
> If I devoted fail to save my offspring.''

Every portion of this prayer, uttered under peculiar circumstances, is admissible, and if the most critical (clerical) observer was to find fault, it would be while she hesitates about committing a sin thus — " doing evil that good may come.'' (Romans iii. 8.)

In Othello, there is one scene which always struck us as being inimical to Christian observance, and might, we think, be omitted; it is where Othello, in the whirlwind of his passion and revenge, urged on by the cursed arts of Iago, maddened to fury, exclaims:

> " Now, by yon marble heaven, (*kneels*)
> In due rev'rence of a sacred vow,
> I here engage my words."

This is the " due reverence " to the bloody deed he contemplates.

> " Even so my bloody thoughts, with violent pace
> Shall ne'er look back, ne'er ebb to humble love,
> Till that a capable and wild revenge
> Swallow them up."

Iago kneels beside him, and perhaps a more master-stroke of hypocrisy is not to be found in the whole range of the drama, and the profanity is overlooked in the delight of the audience, who universally laugh at his audacity, while they execrate his duplicity. He says:

> " Do not rise yet.
> Witness, ye ever burning lights above;
> Ye elements that clip us round about !
> Witness, that here Iago, etc."

Some objection has been made by divines against that passage in Othello which is generally called the drunken scene. Cassio says: " Heaven 's above all : and there be souls that must be saved, and there be

souls that must not be saved." "Forgive us our
sins, etc." The last is a part of the Lord's prayer,
and, uttered under the circumstances of a debauch,
its propriety can the more readily be questioned. To
the actual language itself we do not find fault, but
the incidents of the scene are such, and, worked up
by the actor, the effect it has upon a portion of the
audience is ludicrous, and generally causes laughter.

The hypocrisy of Richard III., in deceiving the
clergy (Act iii. Scene 7), is, perhaps, one of the most
consummate pieces of acting on record. It is to be regretted, however, that the author brought the ministers
of the church of Christ to aid the designing villain.
After accomplishing his wily purpose,— the obtaining
of the crown, — Buckingham salutes him with this
royal title,

"Long live King Richard, England's worthy king,"

and then exclaims :

"To-morrow, may it please you to be crown'd ?"

Gloster replies, in a meek and humble tone :

"Even when you please, for you will have it so."

Buckingham replies :

"To-morrow, then, we will attend your grace :
And so, most joyfully, we take our leave."
[*Buckingham and citizens retire.*]

Gloster, turning to the duped bishops, says :

"Come, let us to our holy work again."

There is a scene in " Such Things Are," which demands attention in this place : Elvirus (Act ii. Scene 3) is discovered watching an old man, who is asleep. The keeper and Mr. Haswell (who is meant to represent the philanthropist Howard) enter.

Keeper.— " That young man you see there, watching his aged father as he sleeps, by the help of fees gains his admission — and he never quits the place, except to go and purchase cordials for the old man (though healthy and strong when he first became a prisoner), is now become ill and languid. See how the youth holds his father's hand ! I have sometimes caught him bathing it with tears."

Elvirus sees them, comes forward, and after some conversation, says to Haswell :

" Behold my father ! but three months has he been confined here ; and yet — unless he breathes a purer air — O, if you have influence at court, sir, pray represent what passes in this dreary prison — what passes in my heart. My supplication is to remain a prisoner here, while my father, released, shall be permitted to retire to humble life ; to serve as a soldier — or in the mines."

Scenes similar to this, in a play intended to " hold, as it were, the mirror up to nature," had they been witnessed by the celebrated John Witherspoon, D.D., would never have called forth from his " *holy* " lips these remarkable words :   " If you go to a play house, you have not only the guilt of buying so much vain communication, and paying people for being wicked, but are also as guilty of going to the *devil's house,* and doing the same honor, as if you was to partake of some heathen festival. You must consider that all the laughter there is not only vain and foolish, but it is a laughter among devils, that you are upon profane ground, and hearing music on the very porch of hell. *Our play-house is in fact the sink of corruption and debauchery.*" Contrast this language with that of an eminent writer of the same period : " The exhibition of dramatic compositions on the stage has, by some of the wisest and best men in all ages, been countenanced as highly serviceable to the cause of virtue."

In the tragedy of " Douglass," we hear Douglass addressing the stars as his Deity — " The glorious stars, etc." Also Jaffier, in " Venice Preserved," swears by " Those twinkling stars, etc." Alicia, in " Jane Shore," says : " And you the brightest of the stars above, ye saints, etc."

In the " Haunted Tower," there is an expression of this character :

" Spirit of my sainted sire."

Perhaps the worst of the kind, take it all in all, is Schiller's " Robbers." One portion of it, we remember, is made up of horrid oaths, profane expressions, and impious thoughts. Charles De Moor in one place makes his friend swear by " the gray hairs of his father." (Act v.) However, as an antidote to this, there is one line from the play which, in justice, we give, as much for its pious thought as its beauty :

' The time has been, when I could not have slept, had I not said my prayers."

There is in the "Mountaineers" another gross outrage on religion and morality. It is where Sadi asks Agnes — "Dost think I am Christian enough yet to venture —" After he has several times tasted wine.

Agnes. — " There is much virtue in good wine.
Sadi. — Nay, an' there be virtue in it — (*drinks*). By St. Francis, Agnes, thy religion is marvellously comfortable.
Sadi. — That must be because my skull is not, yet, altogether Christian."

The dialogue continues in the same strain, and Sadi, after drinking his full, exclaims — " I have two flagons of Christianity within me." There is another irreverent passage spoken by Octavian :

" No — Providence has slubber'd it in haste,
'T is one of her unmeaning compositions, etc."

How different is the use of the word Providence in " The Fashionable Lovers." Aubrey, considering himself as under the guidance of Providence, says :

" All-disposing Providence; who hast ordained me to this hour, and through innumerable toils and dangers, led me back to the affecting spot, can it be wondered at, if I approach it with an anxious, aching heart, uncertain as I am if I have still a child or not."

In the " Surrender of Calais," Providence is also mentioned in a proper manner. La Gloire says :

" What shall we do with our children, Madelon ? "

She replies :

" If your endeavors be honest, La Gloire, Providence will take care of them, I warrant."

The great error of dramatists consists in their blending sacred truth with the fallacies of fiction, and taking the most precious subjects and throwing them into dramatic form with others of a trifling character.

There is in "The School of Reform" a very striking scene, which has always been received with a degree of reverence seldom observed in a theatre. It is a scene between Old Tyke and his son Robert. Robert had led a very wicked life for some years, and had been transported for horse-stealing. He returns, and at length meets with his father, who he supposed had been dead, killed with grief for his son's wickedness. Our readers, at least many of them, are acquainted with the scenes, the interview, and the son robbing the father in the Inn-room — then the discovery, the horror of Robert, his grief, and confession. The old man says that heaven will pardon him. He replies :

" No, don't say that, father, because it can't.

Old man.— It is all merciful.

Tyke.— Yes, I know it is. I know it would if it could — but not me. No, no!

Old man.— Kneel down and ask its mercy.

Tyke.— I dare — father — I dare not ! Oh! if I durst but just thank it for thy life !

Old man.— Angels will sing for joy.

Tyke.— What, may I, think you?   May I — may I?"

[*By degrees he tremblingly falls on his knees, and clasps his hands in energetic devotion.— The curtain falls.*]

There is also another passage equally impressive; it is where Lord Avondale wishes to persuade Tyke to commit a robbery, to secure some papers which he wants. Tyke, whose conversion had now changed him from a low thief to a bright and happy man, hesitates and trembles when the proposition is made to him; his hesitation arises from the somewhat different nature of the robbery, as these papers are very important to his master, and for a moment he is inclined to yield, but his good resolution conquers. Lord Avondale, noticing the trembling of Tyke, asks:

"What alarms you?   No one hears.

Tyke.— Yes, there does.

Lord A.— Impossible.

Tyke.— There does, I tell you — there does.

Lord A.— Ah! how? where?"

[*Tyke, shuddering, points to heaven.*]

In "Jane Shore," Act iv., after Gloster has sentenced her to be turned out into the street to perish, she kneels and prays thus:

"Oh! thou most righteous Judge —
Humbly behold, I bow myself to Thee,
And own Thy justice in this hard decree;
No longer then my ripe offences spare,
But, what I merit let me learn to bear.
Yet, since 't is all my wretchedness can give,
For my past crimes my forfeit life receive;

11

> No pity for my sufferings here I crave,
> And only hope forgiveness in the grave."

In "The Siege of Damascus," Act v. Sc. 2, Abudah, a Saracen, is represented as praying in these words:

> "O Power Supreme,
> Thou mad'st my heart, and know'st its utmost frame!
> If yet I err, O, lead me into truth,
> Or pardon unknown error."

In "Percy" there are several prayers, and as Mrs. More has revised this play, we conclude, had she considered them improper, she would have omitted them. Elwina says:

> "Thou who in judgment still remember'st mercy,
> Look down upon my woes, preserve my husband.
>
> . . . .
>
> Now gracious heaven sustain me in the trial,
> And bow my spirit to Thy just decrees!"   Act v.
>
> . . . "Blest be the fountain of eternal mercy.
>
> . . . .
>
> Oh! Thou Eternal! take him to Thy mercy,
> Nor let this sin be on his head or mine!
>
> . . . .
>
> Receive me to Thy mercy — gracious heaven."
> [*She dies.* Act v.]

There is a passage in Macbeth, though it be not a prayer in itself, yet is an account of one, and is highly beautiful, affecting, and a good lesson. Macbeth is giving an account to his Lady of the murder which he has just committed, and of the conduct of

those who were in the same chamber; and his reflections on his own inability to say *"Amen"* to their
prayers are very fine.

    Macbeth.—"There's one did laugh in his sleep, and one
        cry'd murder!
That they did wake each other; I stood and heard them;
But they did say their prayers, and address'd them
Again to sleep.
    Lady Macbeth.— There are two lodg'd together.
    Macbeth.—One cry'd God bless us! and Amen, the other;
As they had seen me with these hangman's hands,
Listening their fears: I could not say, Amen,
When they did say, God bless us.
    Lady Macbeth.— Consider it not so deeply.
    Macbeth.— But wherefore could I not pronounce, Amen?
I had most need of blessing, and Amen
Stuck in my throat."

Perhaps there is not to be found in the English
language nineteen lines that contain more depth of
reasoning, more fearful presages of the great future,
than the following, when the apostrophizer is on the
verge of committing a great crime — self-destruc-
tion:

          "To die — to sleep —
  No more; and by a sleep, to say we end
  The heart ache, and the thousand natural shocks
  That flesh is heir to: — 't is a consummation
  Devoutly to be wished. To die; — to sleep! —
  To sleep! perchance to dream: — ay, there's the rub,
  For in that sleep of death what dreams may come,
  When we have shuffled off this mortal coil,
  Must give us pause. . . .

> . . . Who would fardels bear,
> To grunt and sweat under a weary life,
> But that the dread of something after death —
> The undiscovered country, from whose bourne
> No traveller returns — puzzles the will,
> And make us rather bear those ills we have,
> Than fly to others that we know not of?
> Thus conscience does make cowards of us all,
> And thus the native hue of resolution
> Is sicklied o'er with the pale cast of thought."
>
> Act iii. Sc. 1.

Shakespeare speaks of prayer as being one of the most important duties man owes to his Maker, and invariably introduces it under circumstances the best calculated to impress its solemnity upon the audience. In but few instances does he permit his characters to utter it irreverently. In " Romeo and Juliet," Act i. Scene 4, Mercutio speaks of one : "Swearing a prayer or two." In such connection it is not only improper, but profane. With few exceptions, however, of which this is probably the most censurable, its use, in upwards of one hundred and fifty instances, is both proper and reverential.

The introduction of prayers on the stage dates back to a very early age, nor have they been confined alone to the pulpit, the stage, and the family circle. Poets and others have invoked Divine aid before commencing their work, thus copying the manner and customs of those who called upon the heathen deities, or the Nine Muses, to aid them in their undertaking.

If Homer, Horace, and Virgil believed in the existence of the latter, and implored their aid in their writings, shall not Christians, believing that it is from God alone that "all holy desires, all good counsels, and all just works do proceed," implore HIS aid?

Milton begins with a heavenly muse, etc.

Pope, in his poem of Messiah, says: "O thou, my voice inspire," etc.

Dr. Young invokes "Heaven's King."

Dr. Johnson, before he sat down to write his "Rambler," by which he intended to instruct as well as to amuse mankind, considered the matter in its true light, and implored the only aid which is effectual. As it is a prayer worthy the man and the occasion, we annex it: "Almighty God, the giver of all good things, without whose help all labor is ineffectual, and without whose grace all wisdom is folly; grant, I beseech thee, that in my undertaking thy Holy Spirit may not be withheld from me, but that I may promote thy glory, and the salvation both of myself and others; grant this, O Lord, for the sake of Jesus Christ. Amen."

11 *

SHAKESPEARE'S USE OF SACRED NAMES IN HOLY WRIT.

"Thou shalt not take the name of the Lord thy God in vain: for the Lord will not hold him guiltless that taketh his name in vain."   *Exodus* xx. 7.

THE name of our Creator, as used by some writers, amounts almost to blasphemy. A learned divine, to whom we are indebted for much information and many important Biblical facts, speaking upon this subject, says:

"When anything, which has at all the semblance of religion, is introduced upon the stage, it is commonly, either a strange mixture of the heathen with the true religion, or often simply heathenism itself. Even Christians are frequently represented as swearing by, appealing to, and putting their trust in the gods; or making deities of virtues; or, after the corruptions of Popery, making their prayers to and putting their trusts in saints and angels."

"It is not improbable, but that an act of Parliament, passed in the reign of King James I. (3d year, ch. 21), 'for preventing and avoiding the great abuse of the holy name of God in stage plays,' hath undesignedly had some part in producing this effect; for writers and performers on the stage, in order to evade the penalty there annexed, or possibly from mistaken notions of piety in some, who, fearing to 'take in vain the name of the true God,' have, instead of that, used the heathen term of the gods, or sworn by some false, or inferior being. Most undoubtedly, the name of God is not to be taken in vain; but surely to introduce it, even upon the stage, with reverence, and in such circumstances as a person in real life ought to use it, is not 'taking it in vain,' is not irreverence, but is a useful lesson and example. The act seems intended to prevent only 'the great abuse of the holy name of God,' and that they should not 'speak nor use the holy name of God,' or of Jesus Christ, or of the Trinity (which are not to be spoken but with fear and reverence), jestingly or profanely. When a pause hath been made before the word is pronounced, and when it hath been uttered with profound awe — surely it cannot be said, that the name of God hath been 'taken in vain,' but that it hath impressed the hearts of the hearers with a similar reverence and awe. Were the same sentiments to prevail in common life, we should not so often hear the blessed names of God and Christ used in common oaths and execrations, nor should we hear the words *good* GOD, and *good* LORD, and many others which might be mentioned, used as common exclamations, on the most trifling occasions." *

The third Act, James I., alluded to, says : "If any person shall in any stage play, interlude, or show, jestingly or profanely use the name of God, etc., he shall forfeit ten pounds." That this statute has been acted upon, appears from Mr. Dibdin's "History of the Stage," in which, speaking of Collier's work, he says : "The stage afterwards was narrowly watched ; obscene expressions in former plays were obliged to be expunged, and nothing new was produced before it underwent the examination of a licenser. In consequence of this many were prosecuted by government for uttering profane and indecent expressions, among whom Betterton and Mrs. Bracegirdle were actually fined." (See also Cumberland's "Rise and Progress.")

With one or two exceptions, to which we have alluded, Shakespeare does not either irreverently or profanely use the word God.† Although freely mentioned throughout his plays, the most sceptical critic cannot condemn the use, or the manner with which it is introduced. The word Deity is mentioned only eight times, as it is evident Shakespeare held that title of the Most High in reverence. The word "Saviour," strange as it may appear to the reader, is only

---

* From a discourse, on "Subjects Relating to the Stage," preached at Great St. Mary's Church, Cambridge, England, Sunday, September 25, 1808, by James Plumptre, B. D.

† In the various editions, heaven is frequently substituted for this word.

mentioned once (Hamlet, Act i. Sc. 1). Allusions, however, are made to him in several passages we have already given. The name "Jesus" is only mentioned once (3 Henry IV., Act v. Sc. 6). Providence is mentioned six times. We have in our parallel passages shown how closely Shakespeare followed the Bible in its connection. (See Hamlet, Act v. Sc. 2.)

That Shakespeare had a due reverence for sacred names, and how in their use he respected them, we have already shown. The Holy Ghost is not mentioned throughout his works, and we can only account for its absence from the fact that it was a word too holy to be used in the common language of the day. Other names of the Trinity can be used without giving offence to religion, but that of the Holy Ghost can only be approached with a due reverence to the mighty power of whom it is an attribute. With this terrible passage staring him in the face, is it to be wondered at that the poet passed it over in awe and reverence?

" Wherefore I say unto you, All manner of sin and blasphemy shall be forgiven unto men; but the blasphemy against the Holy Ghost, shall not be forgiven unto men.

" And whosoever speaketh a word against the Son of man, it shall be forgiven him; but whosoever speaketh against the Holy Ghost, shall not be forgiven him, neither in this world, neither in the world to come." *Matt.* xii. 31, 32.

The word "Jesu" (*Latin*), an abbreviation of Jesus, and introduced as such, is used fourteen times, in a manner we think both irreverent and improper, and contrary to his usual manner of speaking of holy names. As an evidence, we give the passages where the word " Jesu " occurs. The reader will observe that it is uttered more as an exclamation than as a prayer or invocation:

" Fought for Jesu Christ."	*Richard II.*,	Act iv. Sc. 1.
" Jesu preserve thee."	"	Act v. Sc. 2.
" Jesu bless us."	1 *Henry IV.*,	Act ii. Sc. 2.
" O Jesu, my Lord, my Lord."	"	Act ii. Sc. 4.
" O Jesu! I have heard the Prince."	"	Act iii. Sc. 3.
" O Jesu, are you come from Wales?" 2 *Henry IV.*, Act ii. Sc. 4.
" Jesu maintain your royal excellence."	"	Act i. Sc. 1.
" Jesu preserve your royal majesty."	"	Act i. Sc. 2.
" Jesu bless him."	"	Act i. Sc. 3.
" Jesu pardon."	*Richard III.*,	Act i. Sc. 3.
" Have mercy, Jesu."	"	Act v. Sc. 3.
" Jesu Maria — what a deal of brine."		
	Romeo and Juliet,	Act ii. Sc. 3.
" By Jesu, a very good blade." "	"	Act ii. Sc. 4.
" Jesu, what haste."	" "	Act ii. Sc. 5.

With all our admiration of the bard, his profundity, knowledge, learning, and, at times, his solemnity when speaking of Divine things, we cannot but condemn this line from the Second Part of King Henry VI., Act v. Sc. 1 :

" You shall sup with Jesu Christ to-night ! "

Had he substituted any other name beside that of Christ in this connection, no objection could be made, but Richard assumes here a power he does not possess, and is thus aptly answered by Clifford :

"Foul stigmatic, that's more than thou canst tell."

Richard replies:

"If not in Heaven, you'll surely sup in hell!"

The word "Jehovah" is not to be found throughout the works of Shakespeare. The word "Almighty" is mentioned six times, with proper and reverential connection with the text.

Shakespeare uses the word "Christ" nine times. In Richard II., the Bishop of Carlisle introduces it, thus:

> "That honorable day shall ne'er be seen,
> Many a time hath banish'd Norfolk fought
> For Jesus Christ, etc."

In the same scene the Bishop says: "Gave his pure soul unto his captain, Christ;" also, "so Judas did to Christ." In Henry IV. it is mentioned twice, in Henry V. once, in Henry VI. twice, and in Richard III.

In Henry V. there are two characters introduced whose very presence and language are inadmissible,— the latter is particularly offensive,— as they speak in broken English, and make frequent use of the word "Christ," as "by Chrish," and "Cheshu." In one short scene alone in Act iii., these words are used seven times. It is to be regretted that they were eve · brought in at all, for they are of no manner of interest to the play, and their sole business is to swear and use the holy name of Christ improperly. (See *Henry V.*, Act iii. Scene 2, also Scenes 1 and 7.)

The word "Redeemer," is mentioned twice. Richard III., Scene 1, King Edward says they

> " Defac'd
> The precious image of our Redeemer."

The other line, in same scene, the king says:

> " I every day expect an ambassage
> From my Redeemer, to redeem me hence."

The word "Divinity" is used ten times. In "Merry Wives of Windsor," Act v. Scene 1, Falstaff says: "There is a divinity in odd numbers." It is used in some cases with little or no reverence, and perhaps it is well he limited its use to only seven of his plays. In Hamlet, Act v. Scene 2, the word is used so aptly properly, and we may say philosophically, that men of learning have quoted it so frequently as to render it familiar to all. Hamlet says:

> " When our deep plots do pall, and that should teach us,
> There's a divinity that shapes our ends,
> Rough-hew them how we will."

There is a passage in Hamlet where the name of God is improperly used — Act iv. Scene 6. Ophelia, after singing a melancholy air, whose words indicate despair, says: "And of all Christian souls! I pray God — God be wi' you." In this there is nothing objectionable; but in the remark of Laertes there certainly is, where he says: "Do you see this, O

God?" The very question in connection with the scene is not only improper, but is irreverent.

" The subject of prophecy," says a learned divine, " is likewise introduced upon the stage ; sometimes, indeed, seriously, but at other times with great levity and impiety ; but which cannot but tend to increase that indifference, or infidelity and scoffing, which have ever more or less prevailed in the world on this subject."

Witches and conjurors are also introduced, but in these days they are considered merely excitable characters to the modern drama. Shakespeare, how-ever, presents them to us *beings* possessing more than mortal knowledge. (See *Macbeth*, Act i. Scene 5.)

In King Henry VIII., Cranmer, at the christening of Elizabeth, says to the king :

> " Let me speak, sir,
> For Heaven now bids me." Act v. Sc. 4.

He then proceeds to give an account of what is to happen in the reign of Elizabeth and James I.

A similar passage is introduced at the conclusion of the " Royal Convert," respecting the reign of Queen Anne.

In King Lear, Act iii. Scene 2, the Fool speaks a burlesque prophecy. This, however, is omitted on the stage.

> " Henry V. did sometimes prophecy."
> *Henry VI.*, Act v. Sc. 1.

" Henry the VI. did prophecy." *Richard III.*, Act iv. Sc. 2.

12

" He hath a heavenly gift of prophecy."
Macbeth, Act iv. Sc. 3.

" For the testimony of Jesus is the spirit of prophecy."
Rev. xix. 10.

" And they shall prophecy." *Rev.* xi. 3.

" Though I have the gift of prophecy." 1 *Cor.* xiii. 2.

There are numerous other passages in Shakespeare where the use of the word prophecy is truly biblical.

" DAY OF JUDGMENT." This expression is used six times in the Bible, and twice in Shakespeare. 1 Henry VI., Act i. Scene 1, the Duke of Exeter calls it, " the dreadful judgment day," and in Richard III., one of the murderers of Clarence says : " Why, he shall never awake until the day of judgment."

We find in 2 Peter ii. 9, " Until the day of judgment," and in Jude 6, " To the judgment of the great day."

The word sacred is not to be found in the Bible. This may seem strange to those who are not so familiar with its holy contents, yet such is the fact. The word holy supplies its place. Sacred relates to God, or His worship — devoted to religious uses ordained by God — divine, hallowed, etc. Milton beautifully expresses it as " The sacred mysteries of heaven," and " Smit with the love of sacred song." Shakespeare makes use of the word frequently ; we give a few passages wherein it is introduced :

" Dust was thrown upon his sacred head."
Richard II., Act v. Sc. 2.

> " His angels guard your sacred throne."
>> *Henry V.*, Act i. Sc. 2.

> " Holy laws of sacred writ his study."
>> 2 *Henry VI.*, Act i. Sc. 3.

> " Their napkins in his sacred blood."
>> *Julius Cæsar*, Act iii. Sc. 2.

> " The due reverence of a sacred vow."
>> *Othello*, Act iii. Sc. 3.

Shakespeare frequently alludes to Cain and Abel, showing how carefully he studied the Bible, so as to carry out the results arising from the first murder. " To slay thy brother Abel ; " which blood like sacrificing Abel's ; "Spirit of the first-born Cain ; " " Be thou cursed Cain."

The word " gospel," so frequently used in the Bible, is mentioned only once in Shakespeare (Twelfth Night, Act v. Scene 1), " Epistles are no gospels." It is somewhat strange that this word should have been considered so sacred by Shakespeare, while others equally so should have been more liberally used. The word has, however, a holy significance, which may have impressed the bard with a feeling of reverence for its use. The word is derived from God, *Deus*, and *spell sermo historia*. Camden says : " The gladsome tidings of our salvation, which the Greeks call *euangelion*," and other nations on the same word, they call " God-spell, that is, God's speech."

Shakespeare uses the word *gospelled*, as obedient to the precepts of the gospel, as thus in Macbeth, Act iii. Scene 1 :

> " Are ye so *gospell'd,*
> To pray for this good man, and for his issue,
> Whose heavy hand hath bow'd you to the grave
> And beggar'd you forever ? "

LUCIFER is mentioned but once in the Bible.

" How art thou fallen from heaven, O Lucifer, son of the morning."   *Isaiah* xiv. 12.

Shakespeare uses it six times.

" Falls like Lucifer."   *Henry VIII.,* Act iii. Sc. 2.
" Lucifer and Beelzebub himself."   *Henry V.,* Act iv. Sc. 7.
" Prince Lucifer."   *King John,* Act iv. Sc. 3.

Also in Merry Wives of Windsor, 1 Henry IV., and 2 Henry IV.

The word " Lucifer " literally means " light "— " light bringing "—" the morning star "—the name of the planet Venus when she appears in the morning before sunrise. The name of Satan before his fall, and derivatively since his fall, " never to rise again." (*Shakespeare.*)

" The Jews seem here to resume (speaking of the fall of Lucifer, as given above from Isaiah) the discourse, and address the king of Babylon by the title of Lucifer, 'Son of the morning star,' the first in dignity among the princes of the earth ; but he was now fallen from heaven and utterly debased. It may also be applied to the fall of Satan and his angels, as the king of Babylon greatly resembled that arch-apostate in his character and fate." (*Scott.*)

Shakespeare uses the word with no very distinct resemblance to that of its Biblical application. With the exception of the passage mentioned in Henry VIII., his use of it amounts to nonsense; for instance, " Made Lucifer a cuckhold." " His face is Lucifer's privy kitchen," etc.

PRODIGAL. This word is not in the Bible. We are so familiar with the beautiful parable of " The Prodigal Son," that we invariably couple it with the younger son of a " certain man rich and prosperous," who gave him his share of goods, and he departed from his father's house — only to return when all was expended and starvation was staring him in the face. The commentators on this passage give the parable the title of " The Prodigal Son," which has been for ages one of the best moral lessons for youth that was ever written. Let us see how Shakespeare introduces it :

" Story of the prodigal."
Merry Wives of Windsor, Act iv. Sc. 5 ; also,
Henry II., Act iv. Sc. 2.

" A prodigal doth she return."
Merchant of Venice, Act ii. Sc. 6.

" A motion of the prodigal son."
Winter's Tale, Act iv. Sc. 2.

" He that goes in the calfskin, that was killed for the prodigal."
Comedy of Errors, Act iv. Sc. 3.

" What prodigal portion have I spent."
As You Like It, Act i. Sc. 1.

12 *

Blaspheme is used by Shakespeare three times:

> "You do blaspheme the good by mocking me."
>> *Measure for Measure*, Act i. Sc. 5.

> "And does blaspheme his breed."
>> *Macbeth*, Act iv. Sc. 3.

> "You blaspheme in this." *
>> *King John*, Act iii. Sc. 1.

In Holy Writ there are several passages similar to the above, which clearly shows how closely Shakespeare followed the inspired writers, when they had occasion to "check the madness" of the people. As, for instance, "Thou dost blaspheme God," "Blaspheme his name," "But he that shall blaspheme against the Holy Ghost hath never forgiveness, but is in danger of eternal damnation." (Mark iii. 29.)

---

* "I have not instanced in the grossest part of their superstition, not to say downright idolatry, in this kind; I mean on their extravagant worship of the Blessed Virgin and mother of Our Lord, whom they blasphemously call the Queen of Heaven." — *Tillotson.*

THE STAGE, FROM A SCRIPTURAL AND MORAL POINT OF VIEW.

I F our Saviour and St. Paul considered dramas as so absolutely unlawful, so bad in their origin, and so corrupt in their very nature, surely they would not have given their sanction to the instructive sayings of the dramatic writers of old. (See Acts xvii. 28 ; also ix., v., and 1 Corinthians xv. 33.) "Nor is it," says an old writer, "fair to object against the stage. That it hath been abused to the worst purposes there is not a question of doubt. What gift of God, and which of His institutions, have not been so? Hath not even the holy worship, appointed by Himself, been perverted to the exaltation of Baal, Moloch, and the myriad of heathen deities? Hath not the abomination of desolation been set up in the holy place." *

The drama is, in fact, embodied history, brought visibly before our eyes, to afford us examples of bad men to be avoided, and of good men to be followed.

* Rev. James Plumptre, B. D., 1809, Cambridge, England.

It can introduce us to the manners and customs of distant nations, and make us acquainted with places and persons to which we should otherwise be ever strangers; nay, it can go farther, and almost give us the advantage of having lived in remote ages, and profiting by the examples of others, who have long since ceased to be inhabitants of this world.*

To the question of the lawfulness of the stage, must, in a great measure, be involved that of the profession of the stage player. If the stage be in itself unlawful, then not only those who carry it on, but those likewise who attend it, and those who sanction it, become partakers in the sin. But, if the stage be a source of amusement, then the profession is not only innocent, but highly useful and commendable. The only case for doubt appears to be where the stage is considered merely as an amusement, and then, how far it may be lawful for any human being to employ his whole time in subserviency merely to the amusement of mankind, is the question to be determined. One of the strongest objections to the stage made by the clergy in its more remote history, was, " That the performers exercised it for profit,'' or, as it was expressed, " exhibited their persons for hire.'' If the labor be lawful, as we think it is, the laborer, surely

---

* The drama owes its origin, says Aristotle, to that principle of imitation which is inherent in human nature. Hence its invention, like that of painting, sculpture, and other imitative arts, cannot properly be restricted to any one specific age or people.

as well in this as in any other profession, "is worthy of his hire." Luke x. 7.

"Those who devote their time and talents to the service of the public have a right to look for their maintainance from their patrons. Should there, however, be any improper exposure of the person in any of these fictitious representations, for the purpose of raising admiration, or exciting worse emotions, the practice is not only disgraceful, but immoral. If such amusements be vicious, the company are all accessory to the mischief of the place, for if there is no audience we should have no acting." — *Collier*, p. 271.

"We do not contend that a fictitious character on the stage should presume to bring the decrees of heaven into his dialogue for the purpose of making them available for his own or the mere amusement of the audience. If, indeed, in so doing this, other circumstances are added, such as profaneness toward God, or if false morals are taught, or if the persons assembling to hear this lesson had been guilty of immoralities, then these circumstances in themselves are wrong. Abuses, and those grievous ones, no doubt, exist; but, though they have been long attached to the stage, they are by no means necessarily so, and might be separated from it."—*Plumptre.*

The opinion of Addison — the moral and pious Addison — the reformer of the manners of his times, by his elegant and pious writings in the *Spectator,* and the author of the "Evidences of Christianity,"

should go a great way to convince the opponents of
dramatic performances that a theatre, properly conducted, might become a school of morals, and rendered serviceable to the cause of virtue. In No. 446
of the *Spectator*, he says : " Were our English stage
but half so virtuous as that of the Greeks or Romans,
we should quickly see the influence of it in the
behavior of the politer part of mankind. It would
not be fashionable to ridicule religion or its profes-
sors ; the man of pleasure would not be the complete
gentleman ; vanity would be out of countenance, and
every quality, which is ornamental to human nature,
would meet with that esteem which is due to it. If
the English stage were under the same regulations as
the Athenian was formerly, it would have the same
effect that it had in recommending the religion, the
government, and public worship of its country. Were
our plays subject to proper inspections and limita-
tions, we might not only pass away several of our
vacant hours in the highest entertainment, but should
always rise from them wiser and better than we sat
down to them."

The drama appears to be a much more obvious and
natural mode of imitation than either sculpture or
painting, and these, if not taught originally by
Divine revelation, were certainly acknowledged as
lawful, and introduced into the tabernacle and the
temple. St. Luke, it is said, exercised the profession
of a painter, and some of the prophecies in the Book
of Revelation are set forth in pictures. If the great

artist of the tableaux drawn and portrayed on the blue arch of heaven had not been inspired by his Creator to picture truth in tablatures to last through all coming ages, he could not fail to throw upon the canvas of creation those glowing pictures, with burning words, foretelling the coming of our Saviour in all his majesty, power, and greatness !

In the "Exposition of the New Testament," 8vo, Vol. II., page 426, we read : " The generality of these visions, as hath been observed, all are represented under the idea of pictures, portrayed on the leaves of a book. The prophet, therefore, employs picturesque as well as poetic imagery, and hath marked the various figures he hath introduced with such a glow of coloring, and strength of expression, as plainly shows how much his imagination was fired with the original."

The Bible is so perfect, so pure and holy in all its inspirations, which are, in fact, emanations from Deity, that it would be almost sacrilege to compare it with any work that ever came from the brain of man. Yet so perfect is Shakespeare, and so boundless his knowledge and resources, that we may be pardoned in placing his name next to those who made up the " Book of Books."

We have many instances in Scripture of the prophets teaching by actions. See particularly Jeremiah i. 13, 19. Also Ezekiel iv., v., vii. 23 ; xii., xxiv., xxix. 15. Our Saviour's parables were probably, some of them, feigned stories, and some real facts, brought forward as instructive lessons.

There is a peculiar feature in the Bible which leads us to infer that the teachings of the old poets were not overlooked, or neglected by the writers of the Old and New Testaments. Many of the Psalms of David, who died 1015 years B. C., are written in the style of the ode and chorus, which ultimately gave rise to the Greek tragedy. The historians of the stage seem, indeed, to have concurred in ascribing the origin of the drama to the ode and chorus, set to music, and performed in honor of the heathen god Bacchus. So far, perhaps, it may justly be traced to heathenism and to the author of it, but then it becomes an inquiry, whence the heathen stole it, or acquired this ode and chorus in honor of their gods? The probability is that it was borrowed from the worship of the One True God, the everlasting Jehovah, to furnish out idolatrous rites for the abominations of the Gentiles. Certain it is, that the Song of Moses, on the deliverance of the Israelites from their Egyptian oppressors, in the year 1491 B. C., is in the same style of chorus and semi-chorus intermixed. The Song of Solomon is now almost universally acknowledged to have been the Epithalamium, or marriage song, of that monarch, composed on the celebration of his nuptials with the Shulamite, in the year 1014 B. C. One of the greatest adversaries of the stage, speaking upon this subject, says: "The music of the Temple was unquestionably beyond all conception magnificent and grand. Many of the Psalms are little dramas, and were sung in dialogue: a part of the priests answers to their parts, are finely inter-

woven, when at other times all Israel joined in chorus !
Psalm ii.–cxxxv., and many others, are fine specimens
of this sort of poetry. The style of their music was
probably much more solemn and simple than ours, and
the instruments used powerful in a high degree. Perhaps nothing so nearly represented the joys of heaven
above, like the singing of the Psalms of David in the
temple of old.

It is not our intention to speak of the Bible as a
text-book for dramatists, nor endeavor to convey the
idea that the inspired writers had the stage and drama
in view when compiling their great works. Still, they
possess all the elements of the art dramatic, without
the most distant allusion to the stage, which in after
years received the pleasing title of the "Mimic
World."

The biblical story of the "Prodigal Son" is one
of those beautifully told parables with which the Scriptures abound ; it places before us, in a grand picture,
scenes as sublime as they are impressive. It is a drama
told. The opening scene represents the younger son
perishing for want ; he had wasted his substance by
riotous living, and repents of his folly, but, as he
imagines, not past forgiveness from his aged father.
Hope kindling in his heart, he exclaims: "I will
arise and go unto my father ; and will say unto him,
Father, I have sinned against heaven, and before
thee."

The next scene represents his aged father, who, seeing a poor ragged wretch in the distance approaching

13

at a slow and wearied pace — he looks again, recognizes his long lost son, rushes forth to meet him, falls upon his neck, and kisses him. The fatted calf is killed, and there was "music and dancing."

On the 18th of August, 1851, a dramatic version of this parable was brought out at the old Chestnut Street Theatre, under the title of "Azael, the Prodigal Son." The incidents of the parable, as well as biblical observances and costume, were strictly followed, and the splendor of the scene where the son was received, and the "fatted calf" prepared, surpassed anything we ever witnessed on the stage. It was a scene of scriptural grandeur; the moral of the play gave it additional beauty. During the run of the piece, an old friend of the writer, Rev. Theodore Clapp, of New Orleans, was on a visit to this city with his family. At our request, knowing his liberal views, and being an admirer of everything that was beautiful in nature and art, himself and family visited the theatre to witness the drama of "Azael." Well do we remember his words expressed on that occasion. "*The stage,*" said he, "*illustrates Scripture better than the pulpit.*" * We have also found the best and the most moral and religious divines favorable to the stage, and those who oppose it, superficial in education, conceited in opinion, and

---

* Bishop Rundle, quoting Plato's saying, "That if men could behold Virtue, she could make all of them in love with her charms," adds: "A right play draws her picture in the most lively manner." (*Letters*, Vol. ii., p. 108.)

whose *domestic relations will not bear strict scrutiny.*
There are plays in abundance which the most pious
parent may take his children to witness with profit.
Men who have won the highest distinction, not
through their genius only, but for the piety of their
lives, have devoted their talents to writing for the
stage. More than two hundred English clergymen
have been dramatic writers.

There is another of the sacred books, the Book of
Job, which, though it cannot be considered as a
regular drama, yet certainly is written very much in
the dramatic form, as the parties are introduced,
speaking with great fidelity of character, as it deviates
from strict historical accuracy for the sake of effect.
(See *Gray's Key to the Bible.*)

" It is undoubtedly a piece of dramatic poetry ; that
the several answers to Job's pleas make three distinct
àcts, Elihu's reply a fourth, the Deity concluding in
the fifth, the historical parts at the beginning and the
end are a kind of prologue and epilogue, which like
those of the ancients, are plain narrations illustrating
the poetical parts." The opinion most anciently and
generally entertained respecting this book was, that
it was composed by Moses to comfort the Israelites
during their afflictions in Egypt ; and others have
supposed it to have been written by Ezekiel to comfort them during their captivity in Babylon. Now,
although it must be acknowledged that this sacred
poem does not bear the form of a regular drama, and
was not written for the purpose of being represented

by different persons, sustaining the different characters introduced, which must always be considered as
constituting what we mean by the general term,
drama; yet this much we certainly learn from it, that
this form of writing was considered, by persons acting
under Divine direction, as admirably well adapted to
convey moral and religious truths. And though, in
this particular instance, it would have been presump-
tion in any one to have taken upon himself to represent the Almighty or His angels, yet of the other
characters it may be said that if, instead of being read
to the Jews by one person, it had been read by
several: or, if instead of reading, the different parts
had been committed to memory and spoken, as if
they had been considerably increased; and one cannot conceive wherein would have consisted the harm
of thus delivering this lesson, or any other one of
similar character.

Were sacred subjects taken for stage representations, we know of no book more susceptible of
dramatic effect than that of Job; let us take a few
instances: i. 6 — "Now there was a day when the
sons of God came to present themselves before the
Lord, and Satan came also among them."

Let us imagine a stage scene like this: "Deity on
His throne," the sons of God gathering around it.
Satan in all his hellish power and grandeur among
them. The Lord speaks to Satan. They converse.
Light and darkness, good and evil, thus standing face
to face. "Whence comest thou?" are the words

uttered by Deity, when His eyes rest on the enemy of man. Satan answers: "From going to and fro in the earth, and from walking up and down in it." Job is the subject of this interview, and at the suggestion of Satan, Deity is advised to test Job's being "an upright man" by "putting forth his hand," and "touch all that he hath," saying, "and he will curse thee to thy teeth." And the Lord said unto Satan: "Behold, all that he hath is in thy power; only upon himself put not forth thine hand." So Satan went forth from the presence of the Lord.

This, in dramatic parlance, may be called the prologue. What follows? The second scene opens. "When the sons and daughters (of Job) were eating and drinking wine in their elder brother's house." Again the scene changes to Job's dwelling — such a dwelling as Satan describes when he said to the Lord: "Hast not Thou made an hedge about him, and about his house, and about all that he hath on every side? Thou hast blessed the work of his hands, and his substance is increased in the land."

Job, in his old age, happy and contented, surrounded with all that was calculated to make man happy, is one day surprised by the sudden entrance of a messenger with appalling news — "The oxen were ploughing and the asses feeding beside them. And the Sabeans fell upon them and took them away; yea, they have slain the servants with the edge of the sword, and I only am escaped alone to tell thee." While he was speaking, there came also another, and

13 *

said: "The fire of God is fallen from heaven, and hath burnt up the sheep, and the servants, and consumed them; and I only am escaped alone to tell thee." While he was yet speaking, there came also another, and said: "The Chaldeans made out three bands, and fell upon the camels and carried them away; yea, and slain the servants with the edge of the sword, and I only am escaped alone to tell thee." While he was yet speaking, there came also another, and said: "Thy sons and thy daughters were eating and drinking wine in the eldest brother's house, and behold, there came a great wind from the wilderness, and smote the four corners of the house, and it fell upon the young men, and they are dead; and I only am escaped alone to tell thee." *

Then Job arose, and rent his mantle, and shaved his head, and fell down upon the ground, and said: "Naked came I out of my mother's womb, and naked shall I return thither; the Lord gave and the Lord hath taken away. Blessed be the name of the Lord." Job i.

There is not in the whole range of the modern acting drama a scene to equal this — the opening of a great scriptural allegorical play. The greatest affliction, the loss of his sons, was reserved for the last, that it might drive Job desperate, when the hand of

---

* This passage, no doubt, suggested to Shakespeare that inimitable scene in "Macbeth," where he receives the startling intelligence of the approach of the foe, and of Birnam wood moving toward Dunsinane. Act v. Sc. 2, 3, 4.

God seemed to be thus gone forth against him. Let the reader refer to the book of Job, and follow up the scenes of his suffering; the meeting of his friends, their counsels; the complaints of his wife; another assembling of the sons of God, with Satan among them. The restoration of the fortune of Job, so the "Lord blessed his latter end more than his beginning, for he had fourteen thousand sheep, and six thousand camels, and a thousand yoke of oxen, and a thousand she asses. He had also seven sons and three daughters, and in all the land were no women found so fair as the daughters of Job. After this lived Job one hundred and forty years, and saw his sons, and his sons' sons, even four generations. So Job died, being old and full of days."

A very great antiquity is generally ascribed to the book of Job. Some think it the most ancient one on record. The style has likewise induced an opinion that it was written in the Arabic language; perhaps Elihu wrote it in Arabic, and Moses rendered it into Hebrew. Some ascribe it to Job himself, but as it is not written in the style of an autobiography, but rather in that of biography, by a second or third party, this supposition falls to the ground.

Job is supposed to have lived long before any part of the Scriptures was written, but he was acquainted with the truths and will of God, by tradition and immediate revelation, and so he was not a Gentile, at least not a stranger to revealed truth. As an evidence of the book being of Arabian origin, it opens with naming the place of Job's birth: "There was a man in the land of Uz, whose name was Job," etc. The land of Uz was a district in Arabia, to the south of Canaan.

"Ruth" is another of these scriptural dramas. The opera of "Rosanna; or, the Reapers," a popular stage piece, is taken from the story of Boaz and Ruth, and is a beautiful picture of rural love. The incidents are given in the Bible, in almost a dramatic form, and are found in chapter iv. 13, 15, 17, and are in strict accordance with stage observances.

To Shakespeare are we indebted for numerous passages of extreme beauty, and which are incorporated in our language, and have become, as it were, "household words." The pulpit, the bar, the senate, quote from his works with a facility that shows to what extent they are read. The former particularly, not unfrequently, when carried away by the subject of the text, involuntarily quote the dramatist, and blush when accused of the clerical knowledge of the bard. Hereafter, when a speaker wishes to quote Shakespeare, let him first be assured that it is not in the Bible, for we have on several occasions noticed public speakers confounding the profane with the sacred, giving to the former all the pathos and devotion which belong almost entirely to the latter. And yet, why should the clergy blush when accused of quoting Shakespeare? *

---

* An Episcopal minister officiating in one of the oldest churches in this city, assured the writer that *he had never read Shakespeare!*

It is not generally known that the Apostles were well read in the poets. St. Paul, in his address to the Athenians, quotes the words of the dramatic poet Aratus:

" For in Him we live, move, and have our being," as certain also of your own poets have said, " for we are also his offspring." *

St. Paul also quotes the Greek poet Menander, 1 Corinthians xv. 33 :

" Be not deceived, evil communications corrupt good manners." †

Our Saviour also, when enthroned in supreme majesty, makes use of a proverb, used also by Æschylus, Euripides, and Terrene, when he checks the madness of Paul. See Acts xi. 5.

A writer, speaking of the amusements of the people, says: " Laws, institutions, and empires pass away and are forgotten ; but the diversions of a people, being commonly interwoven with some immutable element of the general feeling, or perpetuated by circumstances of time and locality, will frequently survive

---

* Aratus, a Greek poet, born at Soles, in Celicia, is the author of a Greek astronomical poem, entitled " Phenomena," which was translated into Latin, and quoted by St. Paul. He was patronized by Ptolemy Philadelphus.

† Menander, a Greek poet, was born B. C. 342, at Athens, studied philosophy under Theophratus, composed one hundred and eight comedies, and was drowned B. C. 290.

when every other national peculiarity has worn itself out and fallen into oblivion."

The festivals and games of the ancients were of a character that could scarcely be expected to survive the dawn of a more civilized state of society. A certain degree of rudeness, and not unfrequently of coarseness and cruelty, characterized all the amusements of remote antiquity, which, being unrefined by any intellectual mixture, were chiefly calculated to display and invigorate the bodily qualities of the parties who engaged in them.

The dance, which at the present day is so much admired as a diversion, was in its origin a sort of mystery and ceremony. The Jews, to whom God himself gave laws and ceremonies, introduced it in their festivals; and the Pagans, after them, consecrated it to their divinities. After the passage of the Red Sea, Moses and Miriam, his sister, to return thanks to the Almighty for the preservation of the people, and the defeat of the Egyptians drowned in the Red Sea, arranged two great dances, with music. One was for the men, and the other for the women. They danced, singing the substance of the fifteenth chapter of Exodus, and performed a graceful ballet. Miriam was celebrated for her Terpsichorean power, and may be considered the founder of the choral song and the dance. The holidays prescribed by Moses to the Israelites afforded rest and amusement to the laboring classes, a relaxation which afforded them diversion from incessant toil, as well as to strengthen their belief in the Mosaic laws. In a year of twelve moons the following holy days were ordered to be kept: 1. Twelve new moons — twelve days. 2. The feast of the Passover — seven days. 3. The Pentecost — seven days. 4. The great day of Atonement — one day. 5. The feast of the Tabernacles— eight days.

The festivals and games of the ancient Greeks were of a character to excite the imagination without improving the mind. Nor was it until the Grecian drama was introduced that the youth of Athens began to turn their footsteps towards the theatre, and listen to the words of its gifted poets. Æschylus, the creator of tragedy, gave to the stage a series of plays which made the age in which he lived classic. He was also the inventor of scenic pomp; and not only instructed the chorus in singing and dancing, but appeared himself in the character of a player; he was the first who gave development to the dialogue, limit, plot, and incident to tragedy.

It is not our design to give a history of the ancient Greek drama, as it has but little to do with the present subject; we simply allude to it for the purpose of showing that, from the earliest ages, amusements for the people were among the most cherished objects of rulers as well as subjects. The Old Testament is prolific with them, and were considered not only innocent, but essential to promote the happiness of the people. These amusements, however, were composed chiefly of dancing, singing, and instrumental music.

A learned writer of the early part of this century says: "But it is objected that our blessed Saviour never was known to laugh." We are not aware that the Apostles ever alluded to the peculiar and social habits of Jesus; they universally speak of Him as having extensive views, business sufferings, compassion, which would render mirth or laughter incompatible with His great calling. But it is very certain that Christ has mentioned laughter as a blessing: "Blessed are ye that weep now, for ye shall laugh" (Luke vi. 21). And the Psalmist says: "When the Lord turned again the captivity of Zion, then were we like unto them that dream; then was our mouth filled with laughter and our tongue with joy" (Psalm cxxvi. 12). And Bildad, in his expostulations with Job (viii. 20, 21), says: "Behold, God will not cast away a perfect man, neither will he help the evil doers, till he fill thy mouth with laughter and thy lips with rejoicing." The Almighty himself, and the Son, and the righteous of the earth— speaking as we must after the manner of men — are represented in more places than one as laughing the wicked to scorn. (See Psalm ii. 4, xxviii. 13, iii. 6, lix. 8.) Though our Saviour was sometimes indignant at hypocrisy, he says of it what may be taken in a ludicrous light: "Woe unto you Scribes and Pharisees, hypocrites: ye blind guides, which strain at a gnat and swallow a camel" (Matt. xxii. 23, 24). The gnat and camel were both unclean animals amongst the Jews.

" God hath made me to laugh ; all that hear shall laugh" (Gen. xxi. 6). There are many passages of Scripture to the effect " That a merry laugh doeth good " (Proverbs xvii. 22, xv. 13 ; Eccles. ix. 7). At the marriage in Cana, at which Christ wrought a miracle to produce the wine, which maketh glad the heart of man (Psalm civ. 15), probably there was festive and facetious conversation. And at the enter-tainment given on the return of the prodigal, which is a representation of the rejoicing in heaven on the conversion of a sinner, there is music and dancing ; and the father says : " It is meet that we should make merry and be glad " (Luke xv. 32).

In the same manner we must reconcile those differ-ent passages of Scripture which seem to condemn all mirth and laughter, and to enforce seriousness : " Woe unto you that laugh now, for ye shall mourn" (Luke xi. 25). " I said of laughter, it is mad, and of mirth, what doeth it " (Eccles. ii. 2). When we consider those as opposed to the passages which seem to sanction mirth, they can be understood as censur-ing only that which is licentious, profane, or unseason-able. The general tenor of the Christian's character should be seriousness tempered by cheerfulness ; seriousness is his occupation, harmless mirth is the relaxation from it, to recruit his spirits, and to enable him to return to it with increased energy ; for, in the words of Solomon : " To every thing there is a season, and a time to every purpose under the heavens ; a time to weep and a time to laugh, a time to mourn

14

and a time to dance. God hath made everything
beautiful in his time, also He has set the world in
their heart, so that no man can find out the work
that God maketh from the beginning to the end. I
know that there is no good in them but for a man to
rejoice and to do good in his life. And also that
every man should eat and drink, and enjoy the good
of all his labor; it is the gift of God." (Eccles. iii.
1, 4, 13.)

A learned writer in the early part of the present
century, speaking upon this subject, says: " Again,
in the amusements of life, if there be nothing in
them derogatory to the honor of God ; nothing contrary to the duties we owe to mankind, and to the
duties we owe to the animals placed under our care
for our use : if they be not of too expensive a nature,
nor occupy too much of our time, but be merely
taken as a relaxation from labor to enable both the
body and the mind to return to their duties with re-
newed vigor: and, lastly, if they can be made subservient to assist us in moral and religious improvement, then may they be said to administer ' to the
glory of God.' "

"What blessing hath been more abused than that
of strong drinks and wine? We now speak as
Scripture speaks. How few — very few — are temper-
ate as they should be, drinking only for the sake of
health, or to exhilarate the heart, stopping short before the glass of excess. Yet, because this blessing
is daily and hourly abused, shall we prohibit it and

put it away from us? No, it is given to comfort us in our 'often infirmities.' (1 Timothy v. 23.) It is given us to 'make glad the heart of man.' (Psalm civ. 15.) And it is one of the symbols of our salvation. (Matt. xxvi. 26–29.) Let us put away the sin, and when we drink, do it 'to the glory of God.' So LET IT BE WITH THE THEATRE.'' (*A lecture delivered in Cambridge, England, in the year* 1808.)

We think the lecturer who made the stage the subject of his discourse erred in naming wine and the theatre in his comparison. Of the two evils, the former is far the worst, and the millions who have fallen victims to it left millions behind to curse the cause of their miserable and wretched deaths. Theatres have no such records.

It is a question whether the term "theatre" was used in the days of our Saviour in the same sense as we speak of it now. It is mentioned but once in the Bible (Acts xix. 29), and that, too, at a period when such temples were not dedicated to the cause of either religion or morals.

The word theatre, used in the New Testament, has been quoted as an evidence of its being in no manner obnoxious to the disciples or to our Saviour.

We do not take this isolated passage as a text to preach from, and assert that the silence of the disciples upon the subject is a proof of their defence of it. On the contrary, they did not go forth to interfere with the amusements of the people — their mission was to preach " Christ and him crucified." As this passage in Acts has been frequently quoted by the advocates of the drama, let us see how and under what circumstance it is used. The city of Ephesus, the capital of proconsular Asia, was noted in its Gentile state for the idolatry and skill in magic, for the luxury and lasciviousness of its inhabitants. The Apostle Paul, on his way from Corinth to the Passover at Jerusalem, called at this famous city, and preached to the Jews in their synagogue. Paul had fearlessly denounced their worship of images. This gave rise to much offence among the workers in " silver models " of the renowned temple of Diana at Ephesus, with a little image in each of them, which were in great request, both as curious and beautiful ornaments and for idolatrous purposes. In their manufacture, a man by the name of Demetrius, a silversmith, employed a great number of workmen, highly to their emolument as well as his own.

Having convened his workmen, and all others whose occupations were connected with the support of the popular and prevalent idolatry, he thus addressed them (Acts xix. 25) : " Ye know that by this craft we have our wealth." 26. " Moreover, ye see and hear that not alone at Ephesus, but almost throughout all Asia, this Paul hath persuaded and turned away much people, saying : ' That there be no gods which are made with hands.' " 27. " So, not only this our craft is in danger to be set at naught, but also that the temple of the great goddess Diana should be despised, and her magnificence should be destroyed, whom all Asia and the world worshippeth.'' 28. '' And when they heard these sayings, they were full of wrath, and cried out, saying, 'Great is Diana of Ephesus.' '' 29. '' And the whole city was filled with confusion ; and having caught Gaius and Aristarchus, men of Macedonia, Paul's companions in his travels, they rushed with one accord into the *theatre.*'' 30. '' And when Paul would have entered in unto the people, the disciples suffered him not.''

The indignation against Paul and the Christians was so great that, had the people so enraged caught Paul, no doubt he would have been put to death. The ringleaders, therefore, not finding Paul, seized upon his two travelling companions, and rushed with them into the theatre, where the public games were supposed to have been then celebrating, probably intending to throw them to the wild beasts, with which slaves and condemned malefactors used to fight, for the cruel diversion of the people. *And this was the theatre at Ephesus,* erected for no other purpose than that for the display of the most cruel and barbarous exhibitions !

When Paul heard of the dangers of his friends, he was desirous of entering the theatre to speak to the people, being willing to venture himself, in hopes of preserving his friends ; but the disciples, knowing that the enraged mob would not scruple to tear him in pieces, interposed to hinder him. Indeed, some of the asiarchs, or officers appointed from the dif-

14 *   L

ferent cities of Asia to superintend the public games, being friendly to him, sent to entreat that he would not expose himself, as they could by no means undertake to protect him. The better and more orderly portion of the audience prevailed upon the multitude, both inside and outside of the theatre, to disperse ; and Paul and his friends were preserved from imminent danger. (Acts xix. 24 to 41, inclusive.)

There were theatres in the cities of Damascus, Ephesus, Antioch, Corinth, Athens, Thessalonica, Philippi, Alexandria, Jerusalem, and at Rome. Yet in all the travellings of the Apostles, with their unsparing epistles against every enemy of virtue and truth, and in all their withering rebukes upon crime, they do not, by a single syllable, pronounce the theatre immoral.

In addition to the above, we may add a few more extracts from the writings of eminent men upon the subject of the stage. It will be understood, however, that they universally allude to the theatre as a place wherein useful and moral lessons could be conveyed. The Rev. John Styles justly remarks : " The stage is the mirror of a nation's virtue, and the enlightened and polished school of a free people."

Mr. Cumberland, in his account of the " Rise and Progress of the English Stage," says : " It is well known to the learned at what expense the Athenians supported their theatres, and how often from among their poets they chose governors of their provinces, generals of their armies, and guardians of their liberties. Who were more jealous of their liberties than the Athenians? Who better knew that corruption and debauchery are the greatest foes to liberty? Who better knew than they, that the freedom of the theatre (next to that of the senate) was the best support of liberty, against all the undermining arts of those who wickedly might seek to sap its foundation? Socrates assisted Euripides in his compositions. The wise Solon frequented theatres, even in his decline of life; and Plutarch informs us, he thought plays useful to polish the manners and instil the principles of virtue."

Bishop Watson, in his letter to the Archbishop of Canterbury, informs us that "St. Chrysostom slept with Aristophanes under his pillow!"

Dr. Walls, in his discourse on the "Education of Children and Youth," says: "It is granted, that a dramatic representation of the affairs of human life is by no means sinful in itself. I am inclined to think that valuable compositions might be made of this kind, such as might entertain a virtuous audience with innocent delight, and even with some real profit."

Andrew Fletcher, of Saltown, says: "That most of the ancient legislators thought they could not well reform the manners of the people without the help of a lyric, and sometimes of a dramatic poet." (1737.)

The pious and elegant Blair, speaking of Tragedy, says: "As tragedy is a high and distinguished species of composition, so also in its general strain and spirit it is favorable to virtue."

Dr. Hey, in his lecture on " Divinity," speaking of the propagation of Christianity, says : " That any one who was master of the history and antiquities of the early ages of Christianity might form fables out of them, for epic or dramatic compositions, which would be extremely interesting, affecting, and improving."

Dr. William Barlow, in his excellent essay on " Education," in one of the chapters speaking of dramatic performances, acknowledges the profession of any actor to be " consistent with religion and virtue."

The late Wm. B. Wood, for many years one of the managers of the old Chestnut Street Theatre, after his retirement from the profession, published a work entitled " Personal Recollections of the Stage " (1855), speaking of which he says : " It is greatly undervalued by many who do not, or will not, perceive its immediate connection with morals and manners. A defence of the drama is no object of the present work ; nor is such thought necessary, while among the pillars of the stage may be found the names of Dr. Johnson, Milton, Addison, Young, Dr. Moore, Cumberland, W. Scott, Milman, Coleridge, Joanna Baillie, and Holcroft." To which we may add the names of the Rev. C. Maturin, Dr. Gregory, Rev. Dr. Croly, Rev. James Sheridan Knowles, Thompson, Mrs. Hannah More, Mrs. Griffith, Mrs. Jameson, Mrs. Metford, and many others of the most pious of the literary world, who have all contributed to the drama.

Lord Bacon says : " The drama is as history brought before the eyes. It presents the image of

things as if they were present, while history treats of
them as if they were things past."

Marcus Aurelius, an emperor noted for his piety,
says: "Tragedies were first instituted to put men in
mind of worldly chances and casualties. After the
tragedy, the *comedia vetus*, or ancient comedy, was
brought in, which had the liberty to inveigh against
personal vices; being, therefore, through this, her
freedom and liberty of speech, of very good use and
effect to restrain men from pride and arrogance, to
which end it was that Diogenes took the same liberty."

Martin Luther says, in his "Tishgesprahle:" "In
ancient times the dramatic art has been honored by
being made subservient to religion and morality, and
in the most enlightened country of antiquity, in
Greece, the theatres were supported by the state.
The dramatic nature of the dialogue of Plato has
always been justly celebrated, and from this we may
conceive the great charm of dramatic poetry. *Action
is the true enjoyment of life — nay, life itself.*" In
another work he says: "And indeed Christians
ought not altogether to fly and abstain from comedies, because now and then gross tricks, and dallying
passages are acted therein, for then it will follow that,
by reason thereof, we should also abstain from reading the Bible." *

Rev. Dr. Knox, in his "Essays," says: "There
seems to me no method more effectual of softening

* Bell's translation of Martin Luther's "Colloquin Mensalia."

the ferocity and improving the minds of the masses of a great city, than the frequent exhibitions of tragical pieces, in which the distress is carried to the highest extreme, and the moral is at once self-evident, affecting, and instructive."

The benevolent, the moral, and pious Jonas Hanway, in his excellent work entitled, "Virtue in Humble Life," in one of the conversations between the father and daughter, thus expresses his sentiments on the subject of the stage :*

D.— "Those who misspend their time in great cities, I suppose, are as often admonished as we are?

F.— Sometimes from the *pulpit*, sometimes from the *stage*, the last being an advantage we do not enjoy here.

D.— I am told that more *evil* than *good* is learnt at the *playhouse.*

F.— Some plays had better not be represented. Your information is so far well grounded. We are sure that those who *husband* life as they ought, the first object of their concern should be to make their *amusements* tributary to the purity of

---

* Jonas Hanway, a philanthropist, was born in 1712, at Portsmouth, England. He was engaged in mercantile pursuits, as a Russian merchant, in the course of which he visited Persia and other countries; he died in 1786. Hanway was a man of great active humanity; he was the chief founder of the Marine Society and the Magdalen Hospital, and contributed to the establishment of Sunday-schools, and to the improvement of the condition of climbing boys (alluding probably to what we term "chimney-sweepers"). Besides his "Travels in Persia," he published many other works, faulty in style, but benevolent in purpose.

their affections, and their regard to their fellow-creatures under all circumstances. If the stage were well regulated, it would mend the *heart*, as well as delight the *fancy* — it might furnish entertainment for the best Christians and philosophers; and teach us all to *be the good characters represented*. If he who writes a play, Mary, had his mind enriched with faith in the sacred writings, it would add strength and lustre to his genius, and charms to his humanity. And were he to teach the daily lessons we should learn, when the expense is not too heavy for our pocket, our minds might be improved by the *play-house* as well as the *pulpit*.*

D.— I fear those days will never come.

F.— We are always to hope for the best. A skilful writer of comedy, or tragedy, might explore the recesses of the mind, and follow the man not into his closet only, but into every scene which the world might call upon him to act in. Let him interest the heart with regard to both worlds, and mark out in legible characters the most useful parts of life. I think we have so much virtue we should be pleased. Every scene in which wit is made offensive to modesty, or the native tenderness of the heart towards each other, should be totally expunged. You know that the *Christian* precepts admonish us not to suffer any *idle*, much less *impure* words, or unchaste conceits, once to be heard amongst us; shall we permit them on a public stage? We are naturally delighted at the report of *generous* actions. In spite of the weakness of the heart, *envy* herself may be discountenanced; great as our corruption is, we secretly applaud, or openly rejoice, when human nature supports her dignity in the person of him whose praise we hear. In this respect the liberty of the *theatre* is greater than that of the *pulpit*. Invention in no character should be strained beyond the bounds of

---

* NOTE BY THE AUTHOR.— " The exhibition of dramatic compositions on the stage, has, by some of the wisest and best men in all ages, been countenanced, as highly serviceable to the cause of virtue." — *Biographia Dramatica.*

probability ; let everything represented have a foundation in reason and truth, and correspond with the ordinary events of life, as we now find it, and we shall be interested.* *Christian diversions* should be agreeable to Christian duties. The precepts of the gospel do not recommend *insensibility ;* but they restrain the *violence of all passion.* Why should we, being *Christians*, delight to behold the soul tortured with *passion*, which Christianity forbids ? Take real life as we find it, and there is enough of the *marvellous to admire*, while *candor* itself will often excite laughter.

D.— And we may be sure, my father, there is no want of *distress* to make us *weep.*

F.— Real life has, indeed, enough of that. Could we learn from our public shows, as well as common life, how to *live well*, we should not be so ignorant how to *die well.* Whoever shows us our own hearts *uncovered* and fairly laid open, discovers many black *spots* in them ; but let them in charity give also a just view of our good qualities ; this may induce us to be more joyful than we had imagined ourselves capable of being ; and balancing the account, leaving us rich in *hope.* He who is busy to mark but with a malignant eye the characters which disgrace human nature, is as little a friend to humanity as him who flatters with a view to deceive. Compounded as we are, we must take the good and the evil together. Real life is made up of *comedy* and *tragedy.*

D.— Do all kinds of people go to plays ?

F.—You will find many of the middle ranks, as well as the *great*, attend theatrical representations. Some of the former empty their pockets there. Happy would it be were the play-

---

* NOTE BY THE AUTHOR.— Thespis, the founder of the stage, who flourished about 536, before Christ, took for his subjects the historical traditions of Greece, which he embellished by appropriate fictions, an innovation highly displeasing to Solon, the legislator of Athens. " If we applaud falsehood in our public exhibitions," said he to Thespis, " we shall soon find that it will insinuate itself into our most sacred engagements."

house a school, in which we might learn the *manly* and *god-like duties* of giving eyes to the *blind*, feet to the *lame*, bread to the *hungry*, and instruction to the *ignorant*. The religion and learning of a country should determine what the stage ought to be, to mix instruction with amusement. Whether you live to see this happy event or not, you may be sure the play-house shall never do you harm.*

D.— But are there not some very fine and religious senti-ments in plays?

F.-- Many scattered in various parts; but I wish to see the stage so modelled as to unite entirely with the pulpit, and keep us in constant remembrance of the immortal glory of a life to come! Thus our amusement might be sanctified, our time *redeemed*, and no moment of our fleeting hours lost.

D.— This would be glorious indeed; but I am afraid your conceit, though easy to understand, is too exalted to be carried into execution.

F.— Rather say, ill suited to the present corruption of the heart, which prevails among the greater part of our fellow-subjects. We must *never despair.* My notion is far from being impracticable. Plays are sometimes represented by boys at *school.* If any theatrical entertainment is proper for them, it should be such as will give them an early relish for religion, and teach them to discountenance vice and infidelity, and establish all the good truths of Christianity."†

(2d Edition, 4to, Vol. I., p. 214.)

---

* NOTE BY THE AUTHOR.—Nearly one hundred years have elapsed since the above was written, and the writer's children's children have not seen "this happy event" yet. Prior to this, Addison used the following language : "The stage might be made a perpetual source of the most noble and useful entertainments, were it under proper regulations."

Spectator, No. 93.

† NOTE.—The words italicised in this extract are those of the author. We have given them as they are in the original.

MYSTERIES AND MORALITIES.

IN the early history of the drama, the Church attempted to subserve its doctrines by connecting the Bible, then a sealed book to the many, into visible action and English dialogue, but unfortunately it mistook the *dignity* of the drama, and added to their scriptural texts the incongruous accompaniment of profane, and not unfrequently *indecent, buffooneries,* which would not have been tolerated in the most vulgar booth or Bartholomew fair.

Even the revival of literature, when the classic models of antiquity were well known in England, at least to the learned, did not exercise the smallest influence upon their drama, which, struggling slowly and painfully through the different stages of improvement, assumed successively the form of mysteries and miracles, moralities, interludes, masks, until the glorious reign of Elizabeth. This was indeed a brilliant age for the drama. It aroused the public mind from its cloistered slumbers; the genius of Great Britain burst forth at once, and in all directions, but more especially in that of the drama, with an intellectual might, majesty, and effulgence, which have not been paralleled in any age or country.

The attempt of the Church to identify the drama with its ceremonies, did more injury to its projects than ever did the opposition of the clergy in after years. The effect, as might be expected, was a bad one, for the sacred characters of the Bible were ridiculed, and many of the most striking passages turned into burlesque and profanity, to cater for the ignorant and gratify the folly, and we may say wickedness, of the priestly dramatists.

We do not purpose to devote much space to the history of the drama of England, as much of the material for such a purpose is lost in the vortex of its religious and political revolutions. The reader, therefore, will be presented with only some of the leading features of the ancient national stage history, and of the principal points of its rise and improvement.

The old Greek drama appears to have flourished at Constantinople until the fourth century of the Christian era; about which time Gregory of Nazianzen, the Patriarch of that city, a poet, and one of the fathers of the Church, banished the pagan plays of Sophocles and Euripides from the stage, and introduced those Scripture histories which appear to have been the earliest dramatic entertainments in every part of Europe.* In these the Grecian choruses were

---

* In banishing " the pagan plays of Sophocles and Euri-

turned into Christian hymns, the pieces being arranged on the plan of the more ancient tragedies; and one of the oldest religious dramas written by Gregory is yet extant, called "Christ's Passion," the prologue to which states, that the Virgin Mary was then for the first time brought upon the stage. The early commercial intercourse between Constantinople and Italy, soon introduced these performances into Europe; in which country the Italian theatre is affirmed to be the most ancient. The period of its earliest religious drama is, nevertheless, assigned to the year 1243, when a spiritual comedy was performed at Padua; and in 1264, the Fraternitate del Gonfalóne was established, part of whose occupation was to represent the sufferings of Christ during Pas-

---

pides," and substituting plays founded upon scriptural subjects, the question naturally arises, was the stage benefited by the change? The founder of the stage, who flourished about 536 B. C., took for his subjects the historical traditions of Greece, which he embellished by appropriate fictions, an innovation highly displeasing to Solon, the legislator of Athens. Æschylus, Sophocles, and Euripides became the great reformers of the Grecian stage — they introduced a number of characters in their plays, perfected their costumes and scenic illusions, banished murders from the stage, and restricted the functions of the chorus, thus rendering the drama worthy the classic age in which it originated. Thus the "Pagan plays" of these great writers laid the foundation of that splendid superstructure upon which Shakespeare devoted a lifetime to embellish and adorn, and whose classic pillars sustain the temples of the histrionic muse, in every land wherever the foot of civilization treads.

sion-Week. The origin of the French theatre cannot be traced higher then 1398, when " The Mystery of the Passion " was represented at Saint-Maur. In England, however, the first spectacle of the kind was probably the miracle-play of " Saint Catherine," mentioned by Matthew Paris as having been written by Geoffrey, a Norman, afterwards abbot of St. Albans, and performed at Dunstaple Abbey, in the year 1110. It is also stated in the " Description of the most noble City of London," composed by William Fitz Stephen, a monk of Canterbury, about 1174, in treating of the ordinary diversions of the inhabitants of the metropolis, that " instead of the common interludes belonging to theatres, they have plays of a more holy character, representations of those sacred miracles which the holy confessors wrought, or of those sufferings wherein the glorious constancy of the martyrs did appear."

It will be hence observed that the ancient religious dramas were distinguished by the names of " Mysteries," properly so called, wherein were exhibited some of the mysteries or events of Scripture story ; and " Miracles," which were of the nature of tragedy, representing the acts or martyrdom of a saint of the church. The introduction of this species of amusement into England has been attributed to the pilgrims who went to the Holy Land ; and the very general custom of performing such pieces at festivals, to the sacred plays at those ancient national marts by which the commerce of Europe was principally supported.

15 *

To these, the merchants who frequented them used every art to draw the people, employing jugglers, buffoons, and minstrels, to attract and entertain them. By degrees, however, the clergy, observing the disposition to idleness and festivity which was thus introduced, substituted their dramatic legends and histories from the Scriptures, for the ordinary profane amusements ; causing them to be acted by monks in the principal churches and cathedrals at certain seasons, with all the attraction and state of choral chanting, playing upon organs, and ecclesiastical dresses and ornaments. The duration of the exhibition appears to have been regulated partly by the length of time appointed for the fair or festival ; for though some pieces consisted of a single subject only, as "The Conversion of St. Paul," or "The Casting out of the Evil Spirits from Mary Magdalene," others comprised a long series of scriptural histories, which were presented for several days successively. The principal of these religious plays appear to have been derived from two very celebrated series of them, annually performed at Chester, at Whitsuntide, and sometimes at Midsummer, and at Coventry at the feast of Corpus Christi, on June 14th. The Whitsuntide plays are commonly called "the Chester Mysteries," both because they were translated by Randle Higden, a monk of that city, about 1327, and were originally played there on the Monday, Tuesday, and Wednesday in the Whitsuntide week, so early as 1269. The most popular exhibitions on these days were generally entitled "Ludus

Coventriæ," or the Coventry plays, because they were performed there at that time, as early as 1416, before Henry V., under the direction of the Franciscan friars of the city, to which fraternity their original composition has been attributed. A transcript of them of the fifteenth century is in the Collonian Library, consisting of forty pageants or plays, also extending from the creation to the judgment of the world.

At the times of these performances, great multitudes were drawn from all parts of England to Chester and Coventry, to the great benefit of those cities ; and, as learning increased, and was more widely disseminated from the monasteries, the acting of sacred plays extended from them to the public schools and universities, when choristers, schoolboys, parish-clerks, and trading-companies were employed in their representation. The mysteries, both of Chester and Coventry, were performed by the members of the leading guilds of those cities ; each society retaining to itself a particular portion of the sacred history. Thus at Chester, the tanners represented "The Fall of Lucifer," the drapers "The Creation," the dyers "The Deluge," etc.; and at Coventry, the shearmen played "The Nativity," and the Cappers "The Resurrection and Descent into Hell." The parish-clerks of London were also accustomed yearly to perform a long series of sacred mysteries near West-Smithfield, at Skinners' Wells. On July 18th, 19th,

and 20th, 1390, they played at Clerkenwell before
Richard II., his Queen, and several of the nobility;
and in 1409 they presented a drama extending from the
creation of the world till doomsday,—supposed to be
one of the Chester or Coventry mysteries,—which
lasted for eight days, in the presence of some of the
principal personages of the kingdom. Down to this
time it does not positively appear that a drama upon
any profane subject, either tragic or comic, had been
produced in England; and even the emblematical and
decorative pageants presented to a sovereign were
almost entirely scriptural. In 1487, after the birth
of Prince Arthur, Henry VII. was entertained at Winchester Castle, on a Sunday during dinner, with a
drama called "The Harrowing of Hell," or the tri-
umphant entry of Christ into the infernal world, and
delivering thence the souls of the faithful departed.
It was performed by the charity, or choir, boys of
Hyde Abbey and St. Swithin's Priory, two large monasteries of Winchester; and was one of both the Chester and Coventry mysteries, sometimes entitled "Ludus Paschalis," or the Easter Play, the subject having
been taken from the spurious "Gospel of Nicodemus,"
as peculiarly proper to the festival. These performances, however, had not become common to all persons without some opposition; since, in 1378, the
scholars or choristers of St. Paul's school, presented
a petition to Richard II., praying him to prohibit
some ignorant and inexpert persons from acting the

" History of the Old Testament," to the great preju-
dice of the clergy of that church, who had prepared
it with considerable cost for representation at the en-
suing Christmas.

In 1511, the miracle play of St. George was acted
in a field at Basingborne, and one shilling was paid
for the hire of it on the occasion.

A volume, called the " Ludus Coventriæ," consisting of miracle plays, is said to have been represented
at Coventry on the feast of *Corpus Christi*, the MS. of
which, says Collier, was written at least as early as
the reign of Henry VII. This volume contains forty-
two plays. We give the title of a few of them, to give
our readers some idea of the subject upon which they
treat : " The Genealogy of Christ," " Anna's Preg-
nancy," " Mary's Betrothal," " The Salutation and
Conception," " The Trial of Joseph and Mary,"
" The Birth of Christ," " Christ Disputing in the
Temple," " The Crucifixion," " Christ's Descent into
Hell," " The Resurrection," " Descent of the Holy
Ghost," etc. Some of these plays are not only com-
mon-place, vulgar, and indecent, but actually blasphe-
mous.

The Widkirk, Chester, and Coventry miracle plays
are infinitely worse than those called " Ludus Coventriæ." The first of these is called " Creation of the
World, Rebellion of Lucifer, Death of Abel.'' We
will give a few of the incidents and extracts from
this *religious drama.* `The Deity thus commences :

M

> " Ego sum alpha et O!
> I am the first, the last also,
> One God in majestie,
> Marvelus of mygt most,
> Fader and Son and Holy Goost,
> On God in trinyte."

The work of creation is then begun, with this very
satisfactory prologue, and after the cherubim have
sung, the Deity descends from his throne and goes
out.   Lucifer usurps it, and asks the angels, " Gay
felows, how semys now me?"   The good and bad
angels disagree as to his appearance, but the dispute
is terminated by the return of the Deity, who expels
Satan and his adherents from heaven.   Adam and
Eve are then created in Paradise, and the piece ends
with a speech from Satan lamenting their felicity.
This ends the first play, or the pageant of the collection and expulsion of Lucifer and his adherents.
The second play relates the murder of Abel.   It is
opened by Cain's ploughing-boy, called Garcon, with
a sort of prologue, in which, among other things, he
warns the spectators to be silent.   It opens thus:

> " All hayll, all hayll, both blithe and glad,
> For here I com, a mery lad ;
> Be peasse youre dyn, my master's bad
> Or els the devill you spide . . . . .
> Fellowes, here I you forbede
> To make nother nose ne cry:
> Who so is so hardy to do that dede,
> The devil hang hym up to dry."

Cain enters with a plough and team, one of his mares being named "Donnyng;" he quarrels with the Garcon, because he will not drive for him, after which Abel arrives, and wishes that God might speed Cain and his man. Cain replies unceremoniously, by using an expression of the most indecent and vulgar kind — an expression, when used with us, denotes the one who utters it an unmitigated blackguard. The murder afterwards takes place, and Cain hides himself; then follows this scene:

Deus.— "Cayn! Cayn!
Cayn.— Who is that calls me?
      I am yonder, may thou not see.
Deus.— Cayn, where is thy brother Abell?
Cayn.— What asks thou me? I trow, in hell;
      At hell I trow, he be:
      Who so were thee then myght he se."

Cain, having been cursed, calls the boy and beats him, "but to use his hand," he acknowledges that he has slain his brother, and the boy advises running away, "lest the bayles us take." This is followed by some gross buffoonery — Cain making a mock proclamation, "in the king's name," and the boy repeating it blunderingly after him. Cain sends him away with the plough and horses, and ends the pageant with a speech to the spectators, bidding them farewell forever, before he goes, as he says, "to the devil."

The above may be taken as a specimen of this class of the Widkirk collection of the miracle plays.

In the stage direction to " The Temptation," is the following : " The serpent shall come up out of a hole," and the devil is said to be " walking near Adam and Eve at the same time ! "

As good and bad are mixed up in everything that appertains to the world, so are they in these miracle plays.   Noah's description of the falling flood, in the play of " Noah's Flood," is by no means unpoetical :

" Behold the heavens !   All the cataracts, both great and small, are open, and the seven planets have quitted their stations.   Thunders and lightning strike down the strong halls and bowers, castle and towers."

In the pageant preserved in the appendix to Brand's history of Newcastle-upon-Tyne, a dispute between Noah and his wife is introduced.   When the patriarch has built the ark, the devil tries to prevail upon Noah's wife not to enter it, observing :

> " I swear thee, by my crooked snout,
> All that thy husband goes about
> Is little for thy profit."

And then he gives her a poisonous draught for her husband, which he himself tastes, but does not swallow.   She tells her husband :

> " By my faith, I no reck
> Whether thou be friend or foe :
> The devil of hell thee speed,
> To ship when thou shalt go."

Noah is so provoked that he belabors her lustily.

At the conclusion, an angel appears, and congratulates him on his victory. When they are all on board, the devil pronounces a curse upon the spectators, which ends the performance.

An incident in the fifteenth Coventry play, is well worthy a place in this connection, and we set it down as one of the most beautiful and original in the whole collection. Mary, seeing a cherry-tree, as she and her husband are walking together, longs for some fruit; and Joseph tells her that he who is the father of her child may procure it for her; the tree instantly bows down to her hand.

"Mysteries and Moralities" became the subject of religious controversy; in the year 1542, a statute was passed by Henry VIII. to purify the government from all religious plays, ballads, and songs, "as being equally pestiferous and noisome to the common weal;" permitting them only for the rebuking and reproaching of vices, and setting forth of virtue, if they meddled not with Scripture contrary to the declared doctrine. John Bates's "Comedy of the Three Laws of Nature," 1538 — in reality a mystery — being a disguised satire against Popery, as was also Weaver's "Morality of Lucy Inventus," written in the reign of Edward VI. The performance of "mysteries" was slightly revived with the Catholic religion under Queen Mary; and in 1556 and 1577 "a goodly stage play of 'The Passion of Christ,' was represented at the Gray Friars, in London, on Corpus Christi day, before the Lord Mayor, Privy Council, etc."

16

In the time of Elizabeth these pieces were probably performed only occasionally and privately, by Catholics. The Chester Plays, revived in 1533, wholly ceased in 1600; and the last mystery performed in England is supposed to have been that of "Christ's Passion," in the reign of James I., at Ely-House, Holborn, on Good-Friday at night, before Count Gondamar, when thousands were present. Moralities continued to be exhibited throughout the reigns of Elizabeth and James I., but about 1570 they began to lose their attraction.

In this interval appeared that species of drama called INTERLUDES, or facetious and satirical dialogues, which were commonly played at the festivals held at the Inns of Court. After various alterations and improvements they became MASQUES, the serious parts of which were divided by a ridiculous Interlude, called the "Anti, or Antic-Masque."

The first English piece which appears like a regular comedy, was produced in 1552, by John Still, afterwards Bishop of Bath and Wells. It was acted at Christ's College, Cambridge, and was entitled "Gammar Gurton's Needle," and abounds in familiar humor and grotesque dialogue. In 1561–62, Thomas Sackville, Lord Buckhurst, and Thomas Norton, wrote the tragedy of "Gorboduc, or Ferrex and Porrex," which was exhibited before Elizabeth by the students of the Inner Temple, on January 18th, at Whitehall. It is a specimen of strong old English eloquence, and is probably the first example in the language of a heroic

tale in verse, divided into acts, and possessing the
formalities of a tragedy. Neither of these dramas appears to have been acted at a public theatre, nor was
there at the time any building in London solely appropriated to plays; but the custom of performing
them at universities, etc., greatly contributed to the
drama's improvement, since their members began to
compose pieces on historical subjects, upon the classical model; and it may also be observed that the
principal early dramatic authors were all scholars.
Their taste, however, between 1570 and 1590, produced a number of those sanguinary and bombastic
heroical pieces which were afterwards so much ridiculed: whilst the plot of "Gorboduc," having been
derived from the ancient British annals, similar sources
were immediately resorted to, and those dramas properly called Histories were brought upon the stage.
They consisted of a series of events taken from the
English chronicles, represented simply in order of
time, but without any artful conduct of the fable:
their introduction has been erroneously attributed to
Shakespeare, though the truth is, that every one of
his historical subjects had been dramatized and performed before his time. With more probability their
origin has been assigned to the celebrated "Mirrour
for Magistrates," first published in 1563, in which the
most distinguished characters of the English annals
are introduced, giving poetical narratives of their own
misfortunes. Romance was also now made the subject
of dramatic performances. "The Palace of Pleas-

ure,'' and various other collections of novels, to which Shakespeare, afterwards, had recourse, as well as comedies, in English and other languages, were carefully examined, to furnish matter for the stage.

The precursors of Shakespeare, who were most famous as dramatic authors, were Robert Greene and Thomas Lodge, remarkable for their humorous satire ; George Peele, a flowery and most ingenious poet ; Christopher Marlow, a fine tragic writer, of great state and sweetness in his verses ; Thomas Nashe, a comic author and satirist ; John Lyly, the Euphuist ; and Thomas Kyd, whose works contain passages not unworthy of the best of his successors. These all contributed greatly to advance the improvement and perfection of the English stage ; and though there be many blemishes to be found in their productions, and much affectation and pedantry, an unfettered spirit of true poetry runs through them all, with language often dignified and harmonious, and always nervous. At length, about 1591, the great luminary of the dramatic world blazed out upon England, and began to produce that inimitable series of plays, which, for more than two centuries, have been the delight, the admiration, and the boast of his countrymen. His excellences are numerous and varied, but the charms of his versification, the beauty of his descriptions, the sublimity of his language, his irresistible humor, and the exquisite nature which pervade the whole of his writings,— are perhaps the most striking features of his splendid genius. His time, too, formed the Golden Age of the drama; since the vigorous language and learning of Ben Jonson, the wit and sweetness of Dekker, the thought of Marston, the gravity of the classical Chapman, the grace and comic vein of Beaumont and Fletcher, the copious genius of Middleton, the pathos of Webster, and the easy mirth of Heywood,— formed an assemblage of more dramatic talent than has ever been witnessed in all the years that have since elapsed.

The most illustrious of these was during the reign of Elizabeth, when literature was advancing under the influence of the Reformation, and the works of the British dramatists began to be stamped with that boldness and energy, that graceful simplicity and exquisite nature, which were so entirely their own.* This is the character of "the best words of the best authors;" whilst the coarse jests and gross language which frequently deform some of their finest and most serious scenes, must be attributed to the imperfection of manners, the slow advance of general civilization, and the remains of that rude humor, which introduced its dissolute and profane merriment

---

* Queen Elizabeth, at the request of Sir F. Walsingham, and with the advice of the Master of the Revels, selected twelve performers out of some of the companies of her nobility which used to act before her, as her own dramatic servants, and to be called the Queen's Players. Of these, Robert Wilson, of "a quick, delicate, refined, extemporal wit," and Richard Tarleton, of "a wondrous, plentiful, extemporal wit," were two. This company, sworn as the Queen's servants, was organized in the year 1583.

into even the sacred stories of the Scripture mysteries. Much of the old poetical spirit remained until the civil wars, when the drama was overthrown in the confusion and violence which ravaged the country; and the restoration brought over that French taste which had been so long familiar to the English exiles. The tide of foreign extravagance and obscenity, of unnatural declamation and unmeaning frivolity, was too powerful for opposition, and even Dryden's splendid talents yielded to the vicious fashion; though their lustre continually breaks forth, notwithstanding their prostitution. With more or less of the same characteristics, the English drama was supported by Otway, Southerne, and Rowe; and afterwards by the many excellent comic and tragic authors of the last century. Slowly and gradually it became purified from its dissolute and profane wit, and if at present the talents of the olden time be no longer evident, the immorality attending them has also departed.

The most important event in the history of the English stage, is that which Puritanism caused, which not only upset the constitution, but entirely suppressed plays and play-houses. This event took place on the 11th of February, 1647, at which time an ordinance was issued by the Lords and Commons, whereby all stage players, and players of interludes and common plays, were declared to be rogues, and liable to be punished according to the statutes of the thirty-ninth of Queen Elizabeth, and seventh of King

James I. To this act was an abridgment, which, two days afterwards, was published, for the suppression of stage-plays and interludes. It made five different provisions on the subject : — 1. It declared all players rogues, within the meaning of the 39th Elizabeth and 7th James I. 2. It authorized the lord-mayor, justices of the peace, and sheriffs to pull down and demolish all stage galleries, seats, and boxes. 3. It inflicted the punishment of public whipping upon all players for the first offence, and for the second offence they were to be deemed incorrigible rogues, and dealt with accordingly. 4. It appropriated all money collected from the spectators to the poor of the parish. 5. It imposed a fine of five shillings upon every person present at the performance of a play.

Before the promulgation of this severe ordinance, the performances of the stage had been frequently interrupted, even from the commencement of hostilities between the king and the parliament. Of the several actors at that time employed in the theatres, the greater part, who were not prevented by age, went immediately into the army, and, as might be expected, took part with their sovereign, whose affection for their profession had been shown in many instances previous to the open rupture between him and the people.

The event of war was alike fatal to monarchy and his people. After a violent and bloody contest, both fell together — the king lost his life by the hands of the executioner ; the theatres were abandoned and destroyed, and those by whom they used to be occupied were either killed in the wars, worn out with old age, or dispersed in different places, fearful of assembling, lest they should subject themselves to the penalty of the ordinance, and give offence to the ruling powers. The fate of their royal master being determined, the surviving dependants on the drama were obliged again to return to the exercise of their profession. In the winter of the year 1648, they ventured to act some plays at the "Cockpit," but were soon interrupted and silenced by the soldiers, who took them into custody in the midst of one of their performances, and committed them to prison.

Amidst the gloom of fanaticism, and whilst the royal cause was considered desperate, Sir William Davenant, without molestation, exhibited entertainments of declamation and music, after the manner of the ancients, at Rutland-house. He began in the year 1656, and two years afterwards removed to the "Cockpit," where he performed until the eve of the Restoration. The performance of Davenant's opera of "The Siege of Rhodes," in 1656, is to be looked upon as the first step towards the revival of dramatic performances, and more properly belongs to the transactions of the reign of Charles II. From this period until the present, the English stage has disarmed fanaticism of its power, and identified the drama with the highest order of the liberal arts.